AN INTRODUCTION TO THE SAINTS CHURCH

AN INTRODUCTION TO THE SAINTS CHURCH

BY PETER A. JUDD
AND A. BRUCE LINDGREN

INCLUDING USER'S GUIDE

Christian Education Office
Reorganized Church of Jesus Christ of Latter Day Saints

Copyright © 1976
Herald Publishing House
Independence, Missouri

All rights in this book are reserved. No part of the text may be reproduced in any form without written permission of the author, except brief quotations used in connection with reviews in magazines or newspapers.

Library of Congress Cataloging in Publication Data

Judd, Peter, 1943-
An introduction to the Saints Church.

Bibliography: p.
1. Reorganized Church of Jesus Christ of Latter Day Saints—Doctrinal and controversial works.
I. Lindgren, Bruce, joint author. II. Title.
BX8674.J82 230'.9'33 75-35763
ISBN 0-8309-0154-X

Printed in the United States of America

CONTENTS

FOREWORD 7
PREFACE 9
INTRODUCTION 11
CHAPTER 1 SOME HISTORICAL HIGHLIGHTS 15
CHAPTER 2 BELIEVING IN GOD 31
CHAPTER 3 WE'RE ONLY HUMAN 41
CHAPTER 4 JESUS CHRIST 47
CHAPTER 5 REVELATION 55
CHAPTER 6 SCRIPTURE 65
CHAPTER 7 THE BIBLE 72
CHAPTER 8 LATTER DAY SAINT SCRIPTURES 83
CHAPTER 9 THE NATURE AND PURPOSE OF THE CHURCH 92
CHAPTER 10 ALL ARE CALLED 103
CHAPTER 11 CHURCH ORGANIZATION 115
CHAPTER 12 HOW THE CHURCH LIVES 132
CHAPTER 13 WHERE IS THE WORLD GOING? 143
CHAPTER 14 EVANGELISM 151
CHAPTER 15 ZION 158
CHAPTER 16 STEWARDSHIP 167
CHAPTER 17 WHAT IT MEANS TO BE A MEMBER 178
CHAPTER 18 PERSONAL IDENTITY 185
CHAPTER 19 ETHICS: DECISIONS, DECISIONS, DECISIONS 192
CHAPTER 20 THE SAINTS CHURCH, THE RELIGIOUS COMMUNITY, AND THE WORLD 201
AN INVITATION 208
APPENDIX
Statement of Faith and Belief 210
Additional Sources 216
INDEX 220

(Turn to back of book for User's Guide.)

FOREWORD

We are pleased to introduce *An Introduction to the Saints Church* which is one in a series of special adult resources which we believe will be very helpful to the church.

For some time we have been keenly aware of the need in the church for appropriate introductory literature which conveys the richness of our history and heritage in the light of the call of God in the modern world. At the heart of this concern is the hope and prayer that the church in all of its dimensions may faithfully do the work of Jesus Christ in the world.

The familiar biblical commission, "Go ye into all the world" (Mark 16:14, I.V.) enriched by the beautiful, "Come to Christ, and be perfected in him," of the Book of Mormon (Moroni 10:29) seem to focus for us in the call to the modern church, "I will call you friends, for you are my friends. . . . I called you servants for the world's sake, and you are their servants for my sake" (Doctrine and Covenants 90:8).

For God the world is the object of his love, care, and redeeming action in Christ. In a similar way this becomes the work of the people of God. The world is made up of persons who all have in common the wonder of their creation, and the ever present evidence of their frailty and inadequateness. We find in this text a commendable effort to deepen our understanding of the church, both in its tradition and history and in the modern-day, dynamic world. We trust that it shall be used widely throughout the church for study and for evangelistic inquiry.

Our appreciation is gratefully extended to Brethren Peter Judd and Bruce Lindgren and all others who assisted in the preparation of this text.

The First Presidency

W. Wallace Smith
Maurice L. Draper
Duane E. Couey

PREFACE

For some time there has existed a need for a book which will introduce persons to the basic elements of the Saints Church. This book is an attempt to fill that need.

As the work of preparing the manuscript proceeded, several things became very apparent. First, it became quite difficult to decide what information of all that is available should be included. This book is intended as an introduction. It is hoped that none of the critical things that should be in a book like this have been left out. The appendix directs the reader to additional sources on most subjects.

Second, this book of necessity reflects the views, emphases, and interpretations of the authors. It could be no other way. There is no doubt that had it been written by other individuals it would be different in a number of ways. This book was written during the spring and summer of 1975. Had it been written several years earlier or later it would also have been different. It is important then that this book be seen as the work of individuals who bring their own unique backgrounds to the task.

Third, this book is intended to be primarily informational and secondarily persuasive. Care has been taken to present as objective and accurate a picture of the Saints Church as possible. It is designed to acquaint interested persons with the basics regarding history, belief, organization, and practice of the church.

The contributions of Richard Howard and Joe Serig are recognized with appreciation. They prepared the first drafts of chapters 1 and 14 respectively. The authors also acknowledge with appreciation the many hours spent by persons who reviewed the preliminary drafts of parts or all of this book. Their comments, suggestions, and encouragement helped to improve the final draft and make it representative of a broader range of views. Thanks in this regard are due to Paul Booth, John Cackler, Clifford Cole, John Conway, Duane Couey, Joe Donald, Harry Doty, Harold Downey, Francis Hansen, Lee Hart, Richard Hughes, Judy Judd, John Midgorden, Harley Morris, Joe Serig, Geoffrey Spencer, Beverly Spring, Barbara Thatcher, Kenneth Thornton, and Alan Tyree. Appreciation is also expressed to many others who have unknowingly influenced this book by their contact with the authors over the years.

It is the hope of the authors that this book will assist in bringing other persons into the same fellowship with the living Christ that they have been privileged to experience.

Peter A. Judd
A. Bruce Lindgren

INTRODUCTION

The Reorganized Church of Jesus Christ of Latter Day Saints is a Christian denomination of about 212,000 members. Its headquarters is in Independence, Missouri. The church is officially established in twenty-six countries. More than 90 percent of the members, however, reside in the United States or Canada. The church was officially organized in 1830 under the leadership of Joseph Smith, Jr.*

The church has lived for many years with the burden of a long name that people have difficulty remembering. In 1972 the designation "Saints Church" was adopted as an official abbreviation. A popular term prior to this time was "RLDS" by which the church is still known among some people. To some, the term "Saints" refers to selected persons who are recognized for having made great sacrifices or performed virtuous acts. Saints are often thought of as better than the average person. However, a survey of the New Testament shows that the term had broader

*The founder's father was also named Joseph Smith (Sr.) as also was one of his sons (III). Where the name "Joseph Smith" appears in this book without additional designation, reference is being made to Joseph Smith, Jr., the founder of the church.

usage during the early years of the Christian church. The followers of Christ, members of the church, were all called saints. It is with this broader understanding that the Saints Church uses the term.

All Christian denominations have characteristics in common. They all affirm a belief in God and more particularly in Jesus Christ his Son who came to earth for the purpose of redeeming humankind. The Saints Church is no exception. This affirmation has always been the central and most basic premise on which it stands. Without this belief, the Saints would have no reason for existing as an organization.

Even though certain basic affirmations of Latter Day Saint belief are shared in common with other denominations, they are included in this book in order to provide the reader with a more or less complete overview of the Saints Church. The reader should notice particularly in this regard the discussion of God, humanity, Jesus Christ, and revelation in chapters 1 through 5.

Yet the Saints Church is also different from other churches. It is unique. The task of describing in a complete sense all the ways in which the Saints Church is different would be extremely difficult. This is particularly true because even though all Christian churches believe in Jesus Christ, each one has its own experience with and interpretation of that belief. In spite of this difficulty, it is possible to identify certain distinguishing characteristics of the Saints Church.

First, it has a unique history. The particular struggles and accomplishments, successes and failures of the Saints are different from those encountered by any other group of people. The Saints are proud of their unique heritage and feel privileged to have spent almost one hundred and fifty years to date attempting to respond to God's call to be his people. Some highlights from this history are provided in Chapter 1.

Second, the Saints believe that God has called and commissioned them to assist him in the establishment of his kingdom. A particular feature of this belief is that God's kingdom will be a reality in this world. The Saints refer to God's kingdom on earth as Zion. This belief is discussed most completely in Chapter 15.

Third, the Saints believe that God reveals himself to all persons in all ages. As evidence of this, they accept two books of Scripture in addition to the Bible. These are the Book of Mormon and the Doctrine and Covenants. These Scriptures are seen as compilations of inspired writings by persons who have experienced God at work in their lives and the lives of people with whom they live and work. These two books of Scripture are described in Chapter 8.

Fourth, the Saints believe that God calls all persons to minister on his behalf. One expression of this is the system of priesthood used by the Saints in which responsibilities for the care and nurture of the church are distributed among many people. This system is described in Chapter 10.

Fifth, the Saints believe that God calls us to provide for our own needs as well as contributing to the needs of others. As one expression of the overall principle of stewardship, the Saints Church teaches a law of tithing in which one tenth of all that is left after providing for our needs is given to the church. The principle of stewardship is discussed in Chapter 16.

Throughout its history and in every aspect of its life, the Saints Church expresses a strong sense of commitment to God's purposes. The Saints believe very strongly that the work to which they are called is not just a product of human dreams or imagination.

They are convinced that God has called and commissioned them to the most important task in the world. Although small in numbers they are not deterred from this sense of commission. They live in hope and optimism that stems from assurance that through Jesus Christ God is victorious over evil and is right now establishing his kingdom on earth.

The Saints have always been anxious to share their testimonies with others. They wish that everyone could come to know the Christ who means so much to them. The content of this book represents one attempt to share with others the essence of their identity.

CHAPTER 1

SOME HISTORICAL HIGHLIGHTS

This chapter will describe selected events from Latter Day Saint history in an attempt to give the reader a feel for the historical development of the Saints Church. Certain events have been chosen in preference to others. This is not alone because of their enduring value to our sense of heritage today but because of the rich meanings of those events in their peculiar settings to the persons involved in them.

INITIAL CLAIMS

Some notice should be taken at the outset of the claims that the early Saints made about themselves and their church. Of particular importance are certain early experiences that led to the founding of the church. One way to get at that is to review what Joseph Smith said about the early days of his life and of the church's experience. He founded the "Church of Christ," as it was then called, in April 1830 at Fayette, New York. Until 1838 Joseph Smith made little systematic effort to describe and explain those early events that had shaped the character of the church. In mid-1838 he began dictating to scribes his interpretation and recollections of those events. By early 1842 serial installments of what he had dictated began appearing in the church periodical, *Times and Seasons*, at Nauvoo, Illinois. From those early writings these summary statements can be made:

1) Heavenly messengers revealed to Joseph Smith through a vision he had as a teen-ager that he was to affiliate with none of the existing denominations. In due time the "fullness of the gospel" would be made known to him, and later, through him, to the earth.
2) In September 1823 an angelic messenger informed him as follows:
   (a) The ancient covenant between God and Israel would soon be fulfilled.
   (b) The work preparatory to the imminent Second Coming of Christ soon would begin.
   (c) The time was at hand for the gospel in all its fullness to be proclaimed in power, to prepare a people for the millennial reign of Christ.
   (d) Joseph Smith was being chosen and prepared to be God's instrument to implement the divine purpose.
   (e) Near his home were buried ancient plates on which was engraved the story of some of the ancient aboriginal tribes of the Western world and of their leaders and prophets. In time Joseph Smith would be privileged to find that record and, by the power of God, be enabled to translate it into English.
3) In September 1827 Joseph Smith unearthed the plates and began the work of translation. He was aided by a device variously called "spectacles," "seer stones," "interpreters," but, finally, by 1838, called "Urim and

Thummim" (see Exodus 28:30) by Joseph Smith. He himself never elaborated on the method of translation except to say that he did it by the "gift and power of God." The "translation" was finished by the summer of 1829. A second, refined, printer's manuscript was produced and the Book of Mormon was released from the press of E. B. Grandin of Palmyra, New York, on March 26, 1830. This was eleven days before the church, already established and functioning, was formally organized as the "Church of Christ."* In his historical narrative Joseph Smith described the Book of Mormon as follows:

(a) The story of ancient Americans, the first settlement taking place after the scattering from the Tower of Babel. The resulting civilization endured about 1,600 years or until about 600 B.C. These people were known as Jaredites after their first leader, Jared.

(b) Shortly before the destruction of Jerusalem, about 600 B.C., a second colony migrated to the New World from Jerusalem. This colony later divided into warring factions, and finally fell to ruin early in the fifth century after Christ. The present American Indians are a remnant from one of those factions.

(c) After his resurrection Christ came to America to plant the gospel in all its fullness, the same as was enjoyed on the Eastern continent.

*Changed to "Church of the Latter Day Saints" in 1834 and to "Church of Jesus Christ of Latter Day Saints" in 1838.

The early Latter Day Saints considered the Book of Mormon to be more vital to their lives than a mere historical chronicle of ancient tribes could have been. There were, in that 588-page collection of writings, significant passages, chapters, and even whole books that related those nineteenth-century folk directly to the ancient tribes. But more than this, persons both ancient and contemporary were seen to be related to the soon-to-be-expected return of Christ and the beginning of his millennial reign.

So it was that the early missionaries of the infant church used, as their chief resource for spreading the gospel, the Book of Mormon. From this book they linked ancient saga with vibrant hope for the kingdom of God. So ardently did they use the Book of Mormon that their many critics and enemies denounced it as the "Golden Bible" and the Saints as "Mormonites." Quite unacceptable to the Protestant churches of the day was a new sect naming itself after Christ and using as Scripture a publication other than the Bible. We can more fully understand the Protestant dislike for the early Latter Day Saint faith by realizing that Joseph Smith's credentials in the eyes of his own people related to more than his translation of the Book of Mormon. They also viewed him as the living oracle of God, receiving timely revelations of the divine will according to his faith and the needs of the church at particular, critically important junctures of its experience.

We can see that the Latter Day Saint movement did not begin by breaking away from a specific Protestant church. Rather it laid claim to be exclusively called to build God's kingdom on earth. This purpose and claim were supported by trust in a prophet who (1) voiced the antiquity of the gospel, (2) affirmed the restoration of that gospel in modern times as touching all dimensions of life, both sacred and secular, and (3) persuaded his followers that history was soon to be fulfilled by Christ's return at a particular place (not time).

Having thus alluded to some of the claims and meanings more important to the founding personalities of the Latter Day Saint faith, we now turn to a brief, selective narrative of the experiences of the early church from its beginning in 1830 to the dispersion of the church at Nauvoo in 1847.

THE EARLY CHURCH, 1830-1847

One term that might be used to sum up the impact of much of the early history of the Latter Day Saints is the "authority-alienation syndrome." By this is meant that the hostility of the larger religious community toward the Latter Day Saints' authoritarian claims tended to strengthen within the emerging church their authoritarian style. This in turn engendered a more hostile response from Protestant neighbors, causing the Saints to take an even more judgmental attitude toward society at large. The ultimate result was total alienation, violence, and forcible removal of the Saints from several of their chosen gathering points.

By midsummer 1830 the small band of "Mormonites," as they were derisively called, felt keenly the hostile pressure. In September 1830 Oliver Cowdery, Parley P. Pratt, Peter Whitmer, Jr., and Ziba Peterson were commissioned by their leader to take the gospel to the Indians who had been relocated just west of the Missouri border, near Jackson County. There was a hint in the written instruction that as part of that mission a new gathering point—a city—would someday be established near where those Indians were.

The missionary team left in mid-October 1830 but detoured to Mentor/Kirtland, Ohio. This was to expose Sidney Rigdon, dynamic Campbellite leader of a religious communal group, to the Book of Mormon message. He and over one hundred of his followers were baptized. They brought to their new church a zeal for the practical application of the faith in terms of communal experimentation. From that time forth the Latter Day Saint movement was shaped to a considerable degree by a devotion to community. That is one of its primary marks of identity and heritage to this day. Sidney Rigdon went to New York to meet Joseph Smith. Within two weeks of that meeting the tiny, struggling church in New York was instructed through its leader to move westward to Ohio. The migration occurred early in the spring of 1831.

Other verbal instructions to those early Saints implied that Kirtland was to be an intermediate stopping-off place, and that an even more important gathering center would yet be made known to them. Parley P. Pratt returned to Kirtland from Missouri in May 1831, bringing a favorable report about the possibilities of Missouri as a place of colonization. Fourteen teams of two elders each were commissioned to travel to Missouri. They preached the gospel along the way in order to win a nucleus of souls for the development of the city mentioned earlier. The teams took various routes, arriving late in July 1831.

It was there that Joseph Smith and Sidney Rigdon dedicated places for a temple and a school. Negotiations were made for land purchases. Independence was declared to be the Center Place for the gathering Saints, the New Jerusalem. Soon the call went out for the gathering to begin. Response to the call resulted in over 1,200 members living in Jackson County by mid-1833 on the nearly 2,000 acres of land purchased by that time.

The rapid influx of such a large number of "New England transplants" into an area previously settled by pioneers largely from Kentucky, Tennessee, and the Carolinas was bound to create tensions. The tensions yielded to hostility and the hostility to violence in the light of hot-tempered resistance to bold religious claims of the Saints. By winter 1833-34 the Saints in Jackson County were forcibly removed by mob action. Most of the evicted Saints began a two-year exile in Clay County, just across the Missouri River.

Meanwhile, response to missionary activity continued to enlarge the church elsewhere. By 1834 work had begun at Kirtland on the church's first building for public worship—the "House of the Lord."* The gathering continued at Kirtland, but the national economic panic of the 1830s took its toll in Ohio as well. The church's banking venture collapsed, its press became insolvent, and there was heavy indebtedness incurred in building the "House of the Lord." To further complicate matters, there was a rapid influx of church members looking for jobs. By late 1837 the church at Kirtland was experiencing a major crisis.

In the early spring of 1838 over six hundred Kirtland Saints migrated westward. They went to places in and around Caldwell County, northern Missouri. That county had been created by act of the Missouri Legislature in December 1836 as a sanctuary for the

*Finished and dedicated with memorable day-long services on March 27, 1836; referred to years later as "Kirtland Temple."

Saints who earlier had been expelled from Jackson County. In the previous June the original Clay County settlers, fearful of the swelling numbers of the Saints in their midst, had asked church leaders to take their people elsewhere. Now their joyful reunion with the incoming Kirtlanders caused them to hope for the most prosperous colony yet and, eventually, a return to their dreamed-for Zion. By early fall 1838 over 5,000 Saints had come to their new haven, headquartered at Far West, Caldwell County.

But Caldwell could not hold them. They spilled over into Daviess, Ray, and Carroll counties at a rate that alarmed established settlers. The vibrant promise of community faded when mob violence under the cloak of legal authority forced the flight of the Saints from Missouri under threat of extermination. With many of their key leaders jailed at Liberty the Saints fled Missouri in the winter of 1838-39. Their sad plight was decried by major newspapers in the nation for its brutality and illegality.

Sympathetic people of Quincy, Illinois, wintered the Saints crossing the Mississippi River. By April 1839 Joseph Smith and the other leaders (jailed at Liberty since December) were reunited with their people. Land purchases were negotiated in and around the deserted townsite of Commerce, Hancock County, about forty miles north of Quincy. Before year's end marshy land had been drained, the town had a new name (Nauvoo), and was well on the way to becoming Illinois' largest town. Late in 1839 the first English converts arrived, and by 1846 five thousand had crossed the Atlantic to settle in Nauvoo. They lent the city a cultural diversity that was both rewarding and challenging.

Ironically, some measures designed to insure the

safety, autonomy, and permanence of Nauvoo had the opposite effect. A liberal city charter was pushed through the state legislature. It brought about a centralization of political and ecclesiastical power that, as it was used, created a virtual "kingdom" on the Mississippi. All but very few of the executive, legislative, and judicial posts in Nauvoo were filled by key church leaders.

Doctrinal speculations thrust the church people farther and farther from earthly realities and closer, in imagination at least, to their dream of the heavenly kingdom. The amalgamation of ecclesiastical and political power within the city infuriated and distressed the citizenry at large. Bitter attacks against church leaders came from various Illinois presses, and even from within the church itself. By early 1844 the climate was ripe for violence. On June 27 Joseph Smith and his brother Hyrum lay dead at Carthage, seat of Hancock County. From that time until early 1846 church people in Nauvoo were subjected to a stream of depredations. As a result, most of them, led by Brigham Young and the majority of the Council of Twelve, left Illinois on the trek to Great Salt Basin.

DISPERSION OF THE CHURCH

From then on into the early 1850s there emerged a number of distinct groupings of Latter Day Saints. These groups still hoped for the kingdom of God in their time but for various reasons could not follow Brigham Young. The most important at that time were groups led by Sidney Rigdon (Pittsburgh, Pennsylvania), James Strang (Wisconsin and, later, Beaver Island, Lake Michigan), Alpheus Cutler (Minnesota), Samuel Brannan (California), and Lyman Wight (Texas).

Many of the groupings of early Saints were short-lived. Some underwent radical changes as they passed into the second generation of existence. They usually followed a charismatic leader who sought to gather the whole church into a Zionic community. And they usually denounced the claims of other factional leaders, hoping to unite all factions into one household of faith. What had begun with such high hope and purpose was not apparently mortally wounded. Nor was it hopelessly divided by persecutions, dissent, and dispersion. The dream was still in the hearts of people who would not yield it to history. They looked forward in hope to its fulfillment—if not in them, then through them.

Most of the Nauvoo Saints went West, but hundreds of others were either unable or disinclined to make such a move. Many dispersed to other parts of Illinois, Pennsylvania, Iowa Territory, Canada, Ohio, Wisconsin, where they united with others of like faith. Or they quietly lived out their lives in the towns where they had settled, and hoped some day to find a meaningful expression of their faith. Many followed one factional leader after another as they tried to reestablish connections with what they had come to prize as the gospel of Jesus Christ.

THE REORGANIZATION

Jason W. Briggs found the church in 1841 at the Newark Branch, near Beloit, Wisconsin. After 1844 he followed J. J. Strang and, later, William Smith, younger brother of Joseph Smith. His affiliation with William Smith was prompted by James Strang's espousal of polygamy. It was also prompted by his own feeling that the church should have leadership by a lineal descendant of the slain prophet. To Jason

Briggs in 1851, William Smith was the logical one to insure that possibility until such a one might mature. Then William Smith himself went polygamous, alienating Jason Briggs and others.

Writing in 1875, Jason Briggs recalled that fateful November 18, 1851, on a prairie near Beloit, where he had experienced what he called a vision and revelation. Jason Briggs's document interpreting that experience was distributed to various small settlements of the Saints in Wisconsin and Illinois after members of his own flock had read it and heard him tell about his experience.

The early Reorganization took some of the images projected in this document as central to its own self-image. For example, for many years the fundamental nature of that self-image was negative. This was due to the felt need to proclaim an authority which could be traced to the founder, Joseph Smith, and which could be "proven" on the basis of "correct" interpretation of church doctrine.

The church published and debated vigorously against the claims of other leaders who were trying to preserve the Restoration movement. Also, great emphasis was laid on the need for the prophet to be a direct descendant of Joseph Smith. Finally, there was the conviction that the church should soon be gathered as one in a central location to build Zion.

Zenas H. Gurley, Sr., and his little flock at Yellowstone (Wisconsin) found meaning in Jason Briggs's document when they received it early in 1852. Sentiment grew for the convening of a conference to organize the church. The first conference of this organization met in June 1852 and declared its dissociation from all existing factional groups stemming from the original church at Nauvoo. It maintained the position that the only proper leader would be one descended from Joseph Smith.

THE YEARS 1860-1914

The early Reorganization was thus committed to waiting and planning and hoping for the day when Joseph Smith III, son of the founder, might see fit to lead the church. Several times in the 1850s delegations from the new organization tried to persuade him to become the president. On April 6, 1860, he was ordained to that office at the annual conference at Amboy, Illinois. In his first speech Joseph Smith III told the conference that he totally abhorred polygamy. He thus set the stage for a long and arduous campaign by the church to clear its name of this matter before the world.

A policy of vast importance was Joseph Smith III's official discouraging of the church members in their desire to gather all to one central place. He constantly urged them to build up the church wherever they were and to identify with the needs and problems of their communities. This approach has shaped the church's conception of its Zionic commission. It advocated the building of "community within community" rather than community withdrawn from society, as had been most often projected by the early Latter Day Saints. The gathering impulse has remained a strong force in the life of the church. It has been manifest in specific attempts to reinstitute the Order of Enoch (1870, 1895, 1910, and 1914), a structure fashioned after earlier Latter Day Saint communitarian experiments in the days at Nauvoo.

The Reorganization early reached out in evangelism, sending missionaries to Utah Territory in 1862; England in 1863; the Society Islands, Scandinavia, and Australia in the 1870s; and to the European continent in the 1880s. In this the church was trying to respond to its early commission to share the hope of the gospel in all the world.

Some of the notable developments of the fifty-four-year tenure of Joseph Smith III were the founding of Graceland College, a nonsectarian school, at Lamoni, Iowa, in 1895 (which in 1975 enrolled over 1,350 students); the opening in 1908 of the Independence Sanitarium and Hospital in response to community and church needs for expanded health care services; and the orderly, gradual, low-key return of hundreds of church members to Independence, looking toward the day (1921) when the church might have its official headquarters at the place so long ago designated as the central gathering point. The return as gradual process rather than headlong rush lent stability and congeniality to the enterprise. It resulted in an acceptance that had been neither realized or possible in the 1831-1833 period.

THE YEARS 1915-1946

Space limits what can be said of twentieth-century developments. It is easy to think of the twentieth century as having begun in 1915 instead of 1900 for two reasons:

1. The socio-political-economic trend in the world at large seemed to have reached a watershed.
2. The year 1915 marked the end of the Joseph Smith III era and the beginning of thirty-one years of the presidency of his son, Frederick Madison Smith.

Frederick M. Smith, son of Joseph Smith III, was awarded the Ph.D. in psychology by Clark University in 1916. He hoped to lead the church in some imaginative and bold enterprises related to righting social injustices so prevalent in the society at that time. But Frederick Smith's dream demanded a quality of leadership and, as he viewed it, a highly disciplined leadership team that would work with the efficiency and skill of an army. His efforts to realize these hopes met with disappointment and personal sadness. The period was characterized by worldwide and national preoccupation with problems of two great world wars and the Great Depression of the 1930s. Some of the significant trends of the F. M. Smith era are these:

1. A resurgence in church literature and thought of the dream of the gathering in terms of specific plans, pronouncements, and programs for stewardship communities.
2. Sustained efforts to clarify the principles and work through the conflicts of leadership roles and functions among the quorums and orders of the church, and to mobilize the membership in a more cohesive force.
3. The articulation and attempt to implement two major church objectives—evangelism and Zion building—as the foci around which the expanding energies and talents of the members could be directed.
4. Emphasis on education for the means of realizing church objectives. For example, 1920 saw the start of a new educational program for some of the church's promising young ministry. The program never came to full fruition because of economic and other problems. However, a number of the more able general officers who began service in the 1920s were trained in this program centered at Graceland College.
5. An extension of the church's programs beyond

its capacity to generate and adequately match the needed economic resources. By 1932 this forced drastic curtailment of program and personnel and a stringent campaign for debt reduction, final liquidation of which was accomplished by 1942.

6. Frederick M. Smith was convinced of the significance of Independence in the life of the whole church. He assumed direct management of the church's affairs in Independence through the First Presidency.

THE SAINTS CHURCH SINCE 1946

Since 1946, the church has grown under the leadership of two of F. M. Smith's brothers, Israel A. Smith (1946-1958) and W. Wallace Smith (1958-) who followed him in the presidency.

One remarkable development since World War II is in the agonizing yet exciting growth toward becoming a worldwide church with more universal theological outlook. This process has been marked by the church's moving through cycles of, on the one hand, housekeeping functions (symbolized by church building construction and fiscal, legislative, administrative, and judicial policy revisions), and on the other hand servanthood (illustrated by sharing ministries offered to "the world" with little or no expectation of economic return). These two categories, it should be noted, are not mutually exclusive.

In recent years the church has been encouraged by the leadership toward a more dynamic and positive self-image (body of Christ, rather than the strong century-long emphasis on being anti-Utah Mormon). This has impelled the church to encourage exploration in theology. A prime question has been, "What does it mean to be the body of Christ in different cultures and at particular moments of history?"

The church's determined response to this question has opened an era of learning what it means to be a prophetic church in the world. Early Latter Day Saints felt the role of the prophetic church to be largely predictive, i.e., the church was to discern the evils of the times that pointed to the end of history, the destruction of the wicked, and Christ's Second Coming. But the theological reflections of the 1960s have brought to the Saints a somewhat different perception of the church's prophetic role. Increasingly the church sees its role as trying to understand what it is called to be and do in this particular moment of time. The Saints are aware that the world is constantly in a state of rapid transition and they attempt to be sensitive to the world's changing needs.

The history of the Saints Church since 1966 is the story of a people learning to work out, implement, and restate broad objectives within the framework of that view of the prophetic church. The learning process has been at once enlightening and beneficial. The expansion of the church into more than twenty new overseas areas of the world since 1960 has stretched its cross-cultural capacities far beyond its previous ability to cope or even imagine. The determination of the church to live and order its priorities in line with broad objectives has resulted in formal planning and individual seminars in various theological disciplines, history, sociology, economics, cultural studies, languages, etc. A wide range of publications and programs emanating from those events have marked the tension of the church's rebirth toward becoming a worldwide agent of redemptive ministry at a time of vast social cleavage and rapid change.

CHAPTER 2

BELIEVING IN GOD

The life of the church is grounded first of all in a faith in God. God is the creator and sustainer of the universe, the source of love and light. Our faith in God is primary, for without it we would have no reason to do the things we do or say the things we say.

Yet the idea of believing in God is not accepted by everyone today. It sometimes seems that the present age makes a belief in God unnecessary if not completely foolish. After all, we can cure "incurable" diseases. People can go to the moon. We can build buildings in ever increasing sizes. Knowledge is expanding at increasingly rapid rates. The situation leads many to say, "What sense does it make to talk about God anymore? Isn't the world at a point where we no longer need this kind of belief?"

It sometimes seems that we are independent and have complete control over our lives. Yet, from time to time, situations arise in which we realize that this is not completely true. We are not masters of all we survey. We are dependent on elements outside our control. We may have to answer to other persons, to government, to physical or financial limitations, or to a host of other things. The fact of life itself is something for which we cannot claim credit.

Ultimately, we are all faced with the fact of our own death. Some of these factors can be changed. Others cannot. Nevertheless, we are all confronted with something or someone outside ourselves.

One of the ways to talk about God is to say that he is that reality to which everything and everyone is ultimately answerable. God is the basis or the ground of everything we call real. The question, then, is not, "Does God exist?" It is, "What is the nature of this ultimate reality?" In response, several affirmations can be made.

1. *God is always greater than our knowledge of him.* God is and will continue to be a mystery. We have learned a number of significant things about God. We have learned some things from Scripture. We have learned others from the mature reflections of insightful persons. We have also learned from our own experience of being confronted with that which is beyond us. Yet we still stand in awe of the mystery of God. We seem to have barely scratched the surface of all that is to be known.

Through centuries there have been numerous attempts to "prove" that God exists and that he has certain qualities (e.g. all-knowing and all-powerful). In the medieval period, Thomas Aquinas and Anselm developed proofs of the existence of God which are generally considered to be brilliant. Since then, many other proofs have been developed. At the same time, many other persons, also considered to be intellectually brilliant, have come to the conclusion that God does not exist. How could this be? Have the atheists and agnostics been less intelligent than we have given them credit for? Have the "proofs" of God's existence been false? The answer probably lies elsewhere.

Proofs of God's existence have simply not answered all of the questions persons have asked about God. How could it be otherwise? If we cannot know everything there is to know about God, if our encounter with God is also an encounter with mystery, we cannot expect that the existence of God can be "proven" in the sense that a mathematical formula can. Our encounter with God consists of much more than an intellectual exercise. God encounters us in the wholeness of our being, and the experience of that encounter cannot be fully reproduced by a series of logically consistent arguments.

This is why we talk about *faith* in God. The Scriptures tell us that faith is the "assurance of things hoped for, the evidence of things not seen" (Hebrews 11:1, Inspired Version*). Through faith, we can *believe* in God even though our "proof" is not complete. The apostle Paul said, "For we know in part, and we prophesy in part" (I Corinthians 13:9, I.V. and King James Version). He recognized that our knowledge of God, and therefore our proof of him, cannot be complete. Yet we are not totally lacking in knowledge. We have been encountered by God and have given some expression to that in words. To have faith in God is to realize that some of life's basic decisions are made without the benefit of a logically "foolproof" justification. We marry and bear children without knowing what the future will bring. We choose a vocation without complete assurance that we will find it fulfilling—and often without assurance that there will be a job available. We believe in God and trust him accordingly even though our logical justification is not complete. To have faith in God is to

*See pages 78-80 for discussion of the Inspired Version.

live in uncertainty but with confidence that the future is in God's hands.

This is not to suggest, however, that we should avoid thinking about God in intellectual terms. It is not to suggest that reason should be ignored in reflecting about our experience with God. It is not to suggest that we should act against our better judgment. We must recognize that for human beings there are limitations to what can be known about God. Our encounter with God is also an encounter with the unknown.

2. *God is personal.* In our encounter with God, we are not meeting a reality which is indifferent or hostile to humankind. Impersonal words like "energy" or "force" do not fully communicate the reality that is experienced when we encounter God. We refer to God as "our Father" because the relationship that is experienced with God seems to be most like the relationship experienced between a child and a wise and loving parent. Somehow, we are drawn to using personal terms to express our experience with God.

This is not to say that God necessarily has a physical form like a human being, nor is it to say that God is simply a person who has some extraordinary powers. Rather, we say God is personal because we find that certain personal attributes such as freedom, truth, creativity, love, and beauty are among the basic qualities of reality. To say that God is personal does not say everything that needs to be said about him. At the same time, it is something that *must* be said if we are to say what we mean.

By saying that God is personal, we are saying that those qualities in human beings which make them persons are of ultimate worth in the universe. The purposes of God are being fulfilled where human beings have the opportunity to give full expression to their personal qualities.

3. *God acts in history and reveals himself.* We do not believe in a God who is static or passive. God is involved in a process which has purpose. His purpose is being carried out in the context of human history. It is centered on the love of God for the persons he has created.

With respect to his purpose, we say that God is consistent in his love for persons and his desire that they embody the personal qualities of love, truth, knowledge, goodness, and creativity. God will remain true to this purpose and he acts in history to bring it about. Because he will remain true to his purpose, God retains the freedom to act in ways that will accomplish it. Thus, God was able to send his Son into the world to redeem people even though they had not lived lives worthy of that sacrifice. He sent his Son because of his unfailing commitment to the life of every single person. He continually calls all persons to follow him in faith. God calls persons to trust him, to trust that he will continue to act in history.

Because God acts in the context of human history, his actions reveal something of himself and his purpose. The Hebrews, for example, understood that God reveals himself. They told about their understanding of God and his purpose by telling and retelling the story of their nation and how they understood God to be acting in that history. They told how God acted to free them from bondage in Egypt and how he led them to the Promised Land. Similarly, the Church tells about its understanding of God by telling and retelling the story of how God sent his Son into the world to redeem all people. The Church today continues in those traditions and adds to them by telling and retelling the history of what has happened to it as it has attempted to follow the Christ.

4. *God is the creator and sustainer of the universe.* The book of Genesis presents a dramatic account of how God brought the earth and all of its inhabitants into being. In many circles, consideration of the book of Genesis has centered on whether or not the earth was created exactly as it is told in that book. The question has tended to be, "Is the Genesis account scientifically correct?" This question misses the point. The book was written to answer a much more fundamental question: "Why does anything exist in the first place?"

The Genesis account says that everything exists because God created the world. We did not create ourselves. God created us and we are here for a purpose. The message of the creation story is that we are dependent on God for everything, even for the fact that we exist in the first place. God not only acts in history; he is also responsible for there being a history to act in.

Yet the creation has not ended. As God continues to act in history, he continues to create. He continues to remold and reshape his creation. He is constantly creating a new world with new possibilities and challenges. He continues to renew and redeem his people and to lead them into this new world.

5. *God is love.* Our experience with God leads us to affirm that God is concerned about his creation and that he loves us beyond all measure. God is on the side of his creation and against all that would destroy it. He does not leave us helpless. Love is sometimes difficult to understand. We are often inclined to ask, "If God really loved us, why do we have to live in a world full of pain?" We may remember when, as children, we

were convinced that our parents did not love us because of some restrictions which were placed upon us or because of some pain that we felt. Upon reflection at a later time, we may have realized that what seemed to be a sign of rejection was really an expression of their love for us.

This is not to say that all pain and suffering comes from God "for our own good." Rather, it means that we do not fully understand God and that we cannot always be certain that our immediate reaction to a situation reflects what is really happening.

Our experience with God, especially as he is known through Jesus Christ, indicates that God's love is to be trusted. The apostle Paul says, "If God is for us, who is against us? He who did not spare his own Son but gave him up for us all, will he not also give us all things with him? Who shall separate us from the love of Christ? Shall tribulation, or distress, or persecution, or famine, or nakedness, or peril, or sword? No, in all these things we are more than conquerors through him who loved us" (Romans 8:31, 32, 35, 37, Revised Standard Version).

6. *God is one.* The Church realizes that it experiences God not only as the Father that Jesus talked about but also in the person of Jesus Christ himself and in the Holy Spirit which descended on the Church at Pentecost. Yet Christians believe that there is only one God. These two apparently contradictory beliefs were brought together in the doctrine of the *Trinity*. This doctrine was developed during the centuries following the death and resurrection of Jesus as the Church was attempting to struggle with its experience of God as revealed in Jesus Christ. The interpretation of this doctrine has been a matter of

dispute fairly often in the history of the Christian Church.

Because there is only one God, the affirmations that we can make regarding God must apply to the Son and Holy Spirit as well as to the Father. However, some degree of separation must be made in order to make any discussion of the Trinity meaningful. Jesus Christ as Son of God refers to more than the historical Jesus of Nazareth. It also applies to the living Christ who is experienced in the here and now. Because Jesus Christ plays such a significant role in the church, his significance will be discussed at greater length in Chapter 4.

The Holy Spirit is the living power and presence of God which has been experienced in the lives of persons and of the Church down through the ages. It is by the power and motivation of the Holy Spirit that we can recognize the existence of God and his active presence in the world. Whatever we do in positive response to God's call to be his disciples is done not by our own strength and ability but by his Spirit. The Holy Spirit works in the lives of all persons who open themselves to the power of God. The unexplainable motivation to be caring and compassionate toward others, the pursuit of a more fulfilling life, and numerous other acts are the result of persons allowing the Holy Spirit to work in their lives.

Joseph Smith, first president of the church, expressed what he felt to be the thought of God regarding the Holy Spirit when he said, "Put thy trust in that Spirit which leadeth to do good; yea, to do justly, to walk humbly, to judge righteously; and this is my Spirit" (Doctrine and Covenants* 10:6, May

---

*See pages 88-91.

1829). The apostle Paul refers to love, joy, peace, long-suffering, gentleness, goodness, faith, meekness, and temperance as the "fruit of the Spirit" (see Galatians 5:22, 23, I.V. and KJV). These are the result of the Holy Spirit working in the lives of persons. The Holy Spirit helps us to become the kind of people God wants us to be.

A doctrine or statement of belief is not so much a literal description of reality as it is a way of talking about our experience with God, recognizing that we do not fully understand him.

This doctrine of the Trinity illustrates one of the dilemmas that we face as human beings. We have been encountered by the divine in the midst of our lives. The experience has been significant because we realize that we have been face-to-face with the truly basic reality in the universe. Yet it is extraordinarily difficult to "get behind" that experience and describe it in language which can be readily understood by all. We can only hope that in the telling of our story we can express something of the wonder and the awe of our encounter.

It is important that when approaching the subject of belief in God, or in anything else for that matter, we do not assume that our statements of belief are exact descriptions of the way things are. Each person is a unique and different individual. Therefore, our expressions of belief, the way we view God and interpret our experience with him, will reflect this individuality. There is therefore a sense in which Christians' beliefs are all different although they all profess belief in God. This is evident in this chapter which attempts to capture the common threads of the Christian belief in God. It reflects the mode of thinking, world view, interpretation, and expression of the author. Other persons would express their beliefs in God somewhat differently than what appears here.

For some people, belief in and experience with God is something that is related only to a religious context. For example, we talk about the church sanctuary as the "Lord's house" or as the place where we go to meet God. This should not imply that God has restricted interests and spheres of operation. People over the years have affirmed that God is encountered in the very process of living. We need to come to see God as being active in all phases of life and among all people. God created the entire universe and all that is in it and he judged it good. He maintains a continual interest in what we do in our vocational, family, and social as well as our religious lives. God is found in the seemingly insignificant events of life as well as in the momentous occasions. God is truly everywhere.

Finally let us affirm that our relationship with God is an individual matter. This does not deny our corporate existence but rather acknowledges the personal nature of human beings and of God. This relationship is one of mutual trust and is the basis on which our lives are founded. God extends to everyone the call to follow him. It is up to us to decide the extent to which we will acknowledge our dependence on him.

CHAPTER 3

WE'RE ONLY HUMAN

The book of Genesis says that after God created human beings, he made an evaluation of his creation. "And God saw everything that he had made, and behold, it was very good" (Genesis 1:31, RSV). *Everything*, the book says, was created good, even human beings. What does this mean? The last chapter talked about God; now what about us? What are we like?

It can be said that we, as persons, are good. We have made it possible for millions of people to achieve a standard of living which is much higher than could be dreamed of a century ago. Governments spend large amounts of money on social programs for persons who are disadvantaged. Some of us give to charities which are committed to helping persons with special needs. Some make significant sacrifices, sometimes even to the point of death, so that other people can avoid death or suffering.

At the same time, we can be incredibly corrupt. Polluting our air and water seems to be more economical than finding other means of disposal of our waste. Some of us cannot get enough to eat while others have problems from eating too much. War continues to occur, and it is becoming increasingly more costly in terms of human death and suffering. We treat each other as objects to be manipulated while, at the same time, loneliness is widespread, and we crave fulfilling relationships with each other.

LIVING IN-BETWEEN

Another way to describe ourselves is to say that we are "in-between." We are in between life and death; in between good and evil; in between being autonomous and being members of communities; in between being completely free and being determined by the world around us; in between joy and sorrow. It seems that life is seldom all one extreme or the other.

We are between life and death. Each day carries us farther into life. We grow in our experiences, increase in wisdom, and come to understand life a little better each day. In the sense that we have an ever greater depth of experience to draw from, our lives become richer. Each day offers new possibilities for growth. But while we advance into life each day brings us closer to the day of our death. We never know when death will come, for it is always a possibility. (And, of course, in the long run it is a certainty!) Each day brings us closer to that event.

We are in between being alone and being members of communities. On one hand, we are completely alone. There is a part of me which is just me and no one else. I am autonomous. I make my own decisions for my own reasons. There is a sense in which each of us encounters life alone. No one else can live our lives for us. When it is our time to die, no one else can die for us. We are each unique and separate individuals.

On the other hand, we live in community, relying on other persons—sometimes for little things, sometimes for matters of life and death. We depend on others for almost everything. Our language, values, and behavior are learned through interaction with other persons. Without some kind of relationships with other persons, our lives are incomplete. Dietrich Bonhoeffer, the German pastor martyred by the Nazis, summed up our in-between-ness when he said, "Let him who cannot be alone beware of community. . . . Let him who cannot be community beware of being alone."

We are in between being completely free and being determined by the world around us. We can do almost anything we want to do. Being autonomous, we are free to think about anything we choose. If we decide to be silent about our thoughts, no other person can intrude upon us and force us to change our opinions. Our minds are our own. If we are willing to accept the consequences, we can act upon our thoughts in any way we choose.

However, there is a sense in which we are determined by the world around us. Very early in life, it becomes apparent that certain kinds of behavior are more appropriate than others. Most of the time, we choose to abide by the conventions of our society rather than bear the brunt of sanctions which might be imposed upon us if we depart from them. Being born into a particular culture, we learn to think in particular ways. Certain cultural patterns are accepted as the way things must be. In the United States, for example, it is assumed that cars should be driven on the right side of the road. While we are free, in theory, to drive on the left side of the road, that option usually does not occur to us as a possible mode of everyday behavior.

SEPARATION AND TOGETHERNESS

Because we are in-between, our relationships with life sometimes become strained. At times we find ourselves separated from others, ourselves, and God. At other times, we experience a sense of togetherness and unity. We feel good about ourselves and about our relationships with God and others. There are times and situations in which we are separated from every other person. At its best this gives us the opportunity to examine ourselves and to take a good look at who we are. But sometimes we prefer to be with others. We may feel most lonely when in the midst of a group of other people. Perhaps nothing is as frustrating as being with others and feeling alone and separated from them. Few of us feel apart from others all of the time, however. We frequently experience a kind of closeness to others that assures us that togetherness is preferable to separation. Nevertheless we seem to be unable to achieve the constant unity with others for which we yearn.

Sometimes we are separated from ourselves, surprising ourselves by doing things that we hadn't intended to do. The apostle Paul said, "I do not understand my own actions. For I do not do what I want, but I do the very thing I hate" (Romans 7:15, RSV). Each of us has probably hurt a loved one by unintentionally saying something hurtful or cruel. Occasions like this can lead us to despair. But there are times when we feel good about ourselves. We are proud of our accomplishments and feel that others enjoy our company. We wish it were always this way and that we were never separated from ourselves.

We also find ourselves separated from God. Often this means being in a state of idolatry. That is, we begin to place too much value on our own wants and wishes and lose sight of what is finally most important. Many times we come to the realization that our lives do not reflect what is ultimately important. There are also times when we feel we are in right relationship with God and partners with him in bringing about his purposes. We feel good about these times but somehow are unable to sustain close relationships with God on a continuing basis.

LIVING IN BONDAGE

When we live in separation rather than unity this places us in bondage. We can be in bondage to the past. This can be experienced in feelings of guilt. We are not pleased with what we have done and sometimes feel condemned. Bondage to our past can also result from our refusing to accept change. This puts us in bondage because of our blindness to God's continuing work in history.

We can also be in bondage to the future. Current events may fill us with anxiety about what is to come. Starvation, war, and suffering sometimes seem to be dominating our world. It seems that everything is headed for disaster. Our anxiety about the future can bring us to the point where we are helpless to do anything toward creating a better future.

Finally, we can be in bondage to the present. Our guilt about the past and anxiety about the future can make us unable to respond creatively to the present. The past cannot be changed and the future has not yet arrived. This means, of course, that we can act only in the present. Yet we can be in bondage so that the present is filled with meaninglessness and boredom. Our hands become tied, preventing meaningful action in the present.

RESPONDING TO OUR SITUATION

We find ourselves, then, in the situation of being able to do both good and evil. Instead of always choosing good, we all too often choose evil. This tendency to choose evil is called *sin*.

At its root, sin is rebellion against God. At times, we refuse to accept God's movement in history and resist any kind of change. At other times we refuse to accept God's lordship over history by forcing changes which will be to our own benefit. At still other times we simply refuse to act in ways which help others to live meaningful lives.

Each of these responses to life is an attempt to place ourselves in the center of the universe. They are attempts to replace God with ourselves. We are failing to recognize our finitude and limitations. We do not realize that we are answerable to God.

If this is the case, what are we to do? Our first response must be that of repentance and confession—that is, coming to see ourselves as we really are. It means expressing a spirit of humility. We must take the time to look at ourselves openly and honestly. Without knowing who we are, we cannot hope to become new persons. We must look at ourselves to determine how we are "in-between," separated, in bondage, and sinful.

Second, we can open ourselves to the redemption God has given us in Jesus Christ. God has overcome our sin in the gift of his Son and has given us the possibility of hope in the midst of our despair. This is the good news, the central affirmation of the gospel. It will be developed in the next chapter.

CHAPTER 4

JESUS CHRIST

Jesus Christ is at the very center of our faith. We believe that he is the Son of God who died for our sins and was raised again on the third day so that we might have abundant life. This is the fundamental affirmation of the gospel. Every other affirmation has meaning only in the light of this one. The Saints Church has always witnessed to the reality and significance of Christ.

Paul summed up this central affirmation of the gospel in this statement:

> Have this mind among yourselves, which you have in Christ Jesus, who, though he was in the form of God, did not count equality with God a thing to be grasped, but emptied himself, taking the form of a servant, being born in the likeness of men. And being found in human form he humbled himself and became obedient unto death, even death on a cross. Therefore God has highly exalted him and bestowed on him the name which is above every name, that at the name of Jesus every knee should bow in heaven and on earth and under the earth, and every tongue confess that Jesus Christ is Lord, to the glory of God the Father.—Philippians 2:5-11, RSV.

THE MINISTRY OF JESUS CHRIST

Through the centuries there has been a great deal of controversy about the meaning of the ministry of Jesus Christ. What does it mean to say that Jesus Christ is Lord and that he died for our sin? Just who is this Jesus Christ anyway?

This question could be answered in a number of ways. From a historical point of view we could say that Jesus was a popular Jewish teacher and prophet who was executed by the governmental authorities and who, according to his followers, was raised from the dead. While the story is fascinating, it would probably not be very important except that it somehow had (and continues to have) the power to transform the lives of people. The belief that Jesus died and was resurrected has given meaning and purpose to the lives of millions for nearly two thousand years.

In the centuries which followed Jesus' life on earth, the Church explained this power by using a concept called *incarnation*. This doctrine emerged from a long and complicated controversy about who Jesus Christ really was. It says that in Jesus Christ God took on human form. Jesus Christ was *completely human* and also *completely divine.* Yet he was not simply a mixture of the two; he was not half human and half divine. He was *fully* human and *fully* divine at the same time. His humanity did not make him less divine, and his divinity did not make him superhuman. Thus, Jesus Christ was God incarnate, God in human flesh.

For us today it may be easier to understand Jesus Christ as the "point of connection" between God and humanity. That is, in Jesus we catch a glimpse of what it means to be truly human. In him we begin to understand what kind of potential we have as human beings. At the same time we catch a glimpse of God. Jesus revealed to us the depth of God's love for us and the magnitude of God's purpose in the universe. Somehow this one human being, Jesus Christ, has shown us what it means for us to be human and what it means for God to be God. Thus, he becomes our "point of connection" with God. Through him, we come to understand our relationship to God.

Dictrich Bonhoeffer summarized the life of Jesus by saying that he was the "man for others." Indeed, Jesus' earthly ministry consisted of a series of compassionate acts through which persons were made whole and able to see themselves in a new light. The gospels are full of stories in which Jesus relieved the pain and suffering of persons who were ill or grieved. The gospel according to Luke recalls that Jesus began his ministry by quoting a section of the Book of Isaiah:

> The Spirit of the Lord is upon me,
> because he has anointed me to preach good news to the poor.
> He has sent me to proclaim release to the captives
> and recovering of sight to the blind,
> to set at liberty those who are oppressed,
> to proclaim the acceptable year of the Lord.—Luke 4:18-19, RSV.

As the "man for others," Jesus was continually found among the poor, the sick, and those who were in pain. His ministry can be summarized by saying that he gave of himself to help those around him.

THE CRUCIFIXION

It was in his death that Jesus showed the depth of his concern for humanity. As one gospel writer put it, "He came unto his own, and his own received him not" (John 1:11, I.V. and K.J.V.). Those persons to whom Jesus came did not receive his ministry. Instead, they put him to a terrible death on a cross. The Scriptures make it clear that the crucifixion was not a surprise to Jesus. He could have avoided his fate by abandoning his ministry, but he was convinced that his work was necessary even if it meant his death.

The crucifixion shows both our sin and God's love for us. We are often inclined to feel that we would recognize Jesus for who he was. We often wonder how it could be that even those disciples who were closest to Jesus could have abandoned him at the most crucial time. Yet there is a sense in which we are inclined to do the same. We sometimes treat other persons as objects to be manipulated; yet we are often lonely and crave open and honest relationships with other persons. In these situations, as well as many others, it becomes apparent that we might very well mistake the Son of God for a common criminal and put him to death. As we have seen in the previous chapter, we are in-between. While we are capable of doing very good things, we are also capable of monstrous evil. Perhaps there is no better illustration of this than the fact of the crucifixion of Jesus Christ.

At the same time, the crucifixion is a sign of God's great love for us, a love which is undeserved. Through Jesus Christ, God shows us that he is willing to take all of the pain and suffering we can inflict on him and endure it willingly. He is willing to take our sin upon himself, bear its consequences, and overcome it. Jesus laid aside concern for his own comfort and welfare and took the form of a servant who was willing to take undeserved punishment for our wrongdoing. The crucifixion could have been a reason for God to exercise his wrath. Instead, he raised Jesus from the dead and made his death and resurrection the occasion for our salvation.

THE RESURRECTION

The resurrection is central to our faith in Jesus Christ. It is the event which confirms Jesus as the Son of God and which makes his life meaningful for us. We believe that the crucified Christ was raised from the dead and continues to live as the Son of God.

In many ways the resurrection is difficult for us to

understand. In a modern society such as ours a story about a dead person being raised to life may seem difficult to believe. After all, we are aware that all of us must die. We have all known persons who lived once but who have since died. We do not expect them to rise up before our eyes and return to life. It is something that is not a part of our experience. Yet we proclaim that Jesus Christ died and was resurrected.

Perhaps we cannot understand the resurrection without understanding the community which proclaims the resurrection. After the crucifixion, the followers of Jesus must have been crushed. They had expected Jesus to usher in the kingdom of God, but he had been killed on the cross. It appeared that their cause was lost. In the midst of this despair the disciples were surprised to find that Jesus had returned. He had risen from the dead. The fellowship that had developed during their travels with Jesus began to flourish once more. Through the resurrection, they realized that they had entered a new era. The world had been turned upside down by a marvelous event which had occurred through Jesus Christ. Despair was replaced by joy and hope. Defeat gave way to victory. Life had meaning once again. We cannot explain the resurrection in scientific or medical terms—but we cannot fully explain death either. Through the Scriptures we have the testimony of those who say that they saw the risen Christ. In addition, we participate in the fellowship of the Church, which continues to live because it continues to proclaim the testimony of those first witnesses. The Church testifies to the fact that Christ continues to live and act in the world and that the world is a new place because of his victory over death.

What does all of this mean? Do we simply tell and

retell the story because we find it interesting? On the contrary, the Church continues to proclaim the death and resurrection of Jesus Christ because it finds meaning and purpose in that proclamation. Our proclamation of Jesus Christ is meaningful because we believe that he is our Savior.

SALVATION THROUGH JESUS CHRIST

We live in a time which gives us much in the way of technology, health care, and a high standard of living. Yet our times are also marked by despair, cynicism, and meaninglessness. Our attitude toward life as a society seems to unconsciously reflect what we earlier referred to as sin. In spite of all our good intentions and accomplishments, we are not able to save ourselves. In spite of all of our attempts to find meaning in life, we crucify the one who can give our lives meaning. Because Jesus was resurrected from the dead, we know that God chooses to give us salvation anyway. We cannot find meaning by ourselves, and so God has given meaning to us. We are not able to save ourselves, and so God acts through Jesus Christ to save us.

Through Jesus Christ, God gives us what the Scriptures call *grace*. By saying that we are given grace, we are saying that all our possessions—even life itself—are undeserved gifts from God. Our salvation, our meaning and significance as human beings, does not depend on our own efforts. It is not something which we "deserve" on the basis of our accomplishments. Rather, our salvation comes first and foremost as a gift from God which we do not deserve. God's love for us overcomes our failure to find meaning and significance on our own. God's act in Jesus Christ is his sign that we are loved by God and loved beyond all measure. It is his offering of himself in forgiveness for all that we have or will do.

Because of salvation in Jesus Christ, we have freedom that would not otherwise be ours. We are freed from the futile search to find meaning and significance on our own. We are no longer standing in fear of condemnation and in fear that our lives will be without meaning. Through Jesus Christ, God has declared that we are all his children and that he loves us all with an infinite love. We are freed from the cynical belief that there is no beauty, no truth, no meaning to be found anywhere in life. Instead, we can live in the assurance that we are the recipients of God's love and that he does not forsake us, even in times of adversity.

NEW POSSIBILITIES IN CHRIST

Since we have freedom through thc gospel, our lives are filled with possibility. We no longer need to worry about whether or not our lives have meaning; our salvation is assured through Christ. Therefore, we can concentrate on bringing to pass all of the possibilities which lie before us. We can express our gratitude to God by taking advantage of the possibilities that are ours. We can respond to the gospel in gratitude and participate in the new creation which God is establishing in history.

Our new possibilities in the gospel fall in three general areas. First, we have a new vision of who we are as individual persons. Through the crucifixion and resurrection of Jesus Christ, we are forgiven persons; therefore, we no longer need to live under the cloud of a vague sense of guilt. Through the gospel, we can come to see ourselves as persons who are in the process of becoming fulfilled. Through God's act in Jesus

Christ, we can see ourselves as persons of worth.

Second, we have a new vision of ourselves in relationship to other persons. God's act in Jesus Christ shows us that *all* persons are persons of worth. As a result, we begin to understand that we need and are needed by others. We realize that other persons are in the same predicament that we are in—all sinners who constantly need and receive forgiveness.

We cannot expect all of our relationships to be without conflict. We can expect, however, that broken relationships can be healed. Conflict and disagreement need not lead to totally broken relationships. Our relationships can be redeemed just as our individual lives can.

Third, we have a new vision of the social order through the gospel. Jesus preached about the coming kingdom of God. The resurrection confirms that Jesus' proclamation of the coming kingdom is the truth about the future. The kingdom of God judges the present as an imperfect expression of what it might mean for persons to live together in a society. Through the gospel, we come to understand that God gives us the possibility of living together in harmony and in justice. Like ourselves and our relationships, society can be redeemed and can become a means of human fulfillment.

Jesus Christ is the central figure in the faith of the church. We proclaim that the resurrected Christ is the Lord of the universe and that he gives us the gift of salvation. He is the key to our understanding of God and of ourselves. Furthermore he continues his saving ministry to individuals in every generation and leads in the bringing forth of God's kingdom on earth. Everyone is invited to follow him and assist in this great work.

CHAPTER 5

REVELATION

We have said that God acts in history and reveals himself. This has always been one of the central beliefs of the Latter Day Saint movement. In fact it has been what we might call one of the distinctive emphases of this church. From the formative years of the church the Saints have testified that it is God's nature to continually reveal himself to humanity. The Saints have borne witness to abundant evidences of such revelation in modern times.

A look at the idea of revelation in Latter Day Saint thought will be the focus of this chapter. Several aspects will be addressed. It is appropriate to ask, "*What* does God reveal?" and also, "*Why* does God reveal himself?" Other important questions are, "*How* does God reveal himself?" and "*To whom* does God reveal himself?" In addition, we will discuss the central expression of revelation—*the person* of Jesus Christ. Finally we will look at the ways in which humankind attempts to *respond* to God's revelation.

WHAT AND *WHY* DOES GOD REVEAL?

Human beings down through the ages have continually affirmed the existence of one who is greater than they—whom they call God. Such affirmations have been based on human experience and have always been vital to the religious lives of people. There remains, however, a significant element of mystery in that we are unable to completely comprehend or explain that reality we call God. He is not known by us as a result of our own efforts. Instead we experience God as a result of his making himself known to us. This process of God making himself known we call *revelation.* This means the uncovering or unveiling of that which is formerly hidden. If it were not for God's willingness to make himself known to us we would not know of his existence or anything about his nature and purposes. This benevolent expression by God of himself toward humanity Christians call grace.

Even though God is our creator, and therefore in one sense definitely separate from us, he desires to be with us and to make himself known to us. We are unable to completely understand or explain God because he is greater than we. However, the fact that we have experienced him in various ways is evidence of his desire to make himself known. God wants to be *with* us at the same time that he is beyond us. God makes *himself* known, therefore, so that we can know him, his nature, and his purposes.

In the Bible God is found saying, "Let us make man in our image, after our likeness" (Genesis 1:27, I.V.; 1:26, K.J.V.). Although this statement has been the object of numerous interpretations over the years, it would appear to suggest an appropriate answer to the question "Why does God reveal himself?" If God intends that we reflect his likeness, it seems appropriate that he show himself to us so that we can know him, encounter him, and become more like him. Furthermore, it can be said that God reveals himself because it is his nature to do so. As creator and sustainer of the universe, God keeps in contact with his creation. As with many things about God, we do not fully understand *why* he reveals himself. We just know that he does, because we have encountered him.

HOW AND *TO WHOM* DOES GOD REVEAL HIMSELF?

All this discussion of God revealing himself may seem totally irrelevant to persons who have not identified the influence of God in their lives. Most of us have read or heard of the "mighty acts of God" referred to in the Old Testament. Some of these acts have been couched in what we call the unexplainable, the miracle; one such was the parting of the water for the Children of Israel so that they could escape from the pursuing Egyptians. Other acts have been presented in a more ordinary framework, such as the release of the Jews from captivity in Babylon as a result of the military defeat of the Babylonians by the Persians. These events seem remote from us and from our everyday situations. Many of us say that we just don't have comparable experiences today.

However the Saints have said that God reveals himself not only in such "mighty acts" as those referred to but that he also makes himself known to small groups of people and even to individuals. In the spirit of the apostle Peter, we can say that God is no respecter of persons. He is just as active in the lives of individuals, groups, and nations today as he ever was. God is performing "mighty acts" today among common people like you and me. "This sounds good," we may say, "but he hasn't done anything for me." To see how God has, does, and will act in the lives of people let us now turn to the question of *how* God makes himself known.

The record of human experience contains many testimonies to the effect that God is alive and working in his world today. Some of these testimonies are recorded in Scripture which represents human attempts to record the significant events of God's revelation to humankind. The writer of Genesis affirmed one major point in the early chapters of that book—that God created the universe and all that is in it. God reveals himself through that which he creates. When an artist paints a picture, fashions a sculpture, or composes a piece of music, that artist is revealed in the work of art. It is possible to say something about the artist, the creator, based on what has been created. In the same way, we can say something about God based on his creation. God is revealed in all forms of his creation: in human beings, in other animal forms, in vegetable forms, in mineral objects such as rocks and water. All these represent his handiwork and therefore show us what God is like. Around us we see beauty in flowers, order in the coming of day and night, and initiative and imagination in human endeavor. It is by observing the creation of God that we can know something of his nature and purposes.

God also reveals himself in ways other than in his creative activity. The "mighty acts" of the Old Testament already referred to testify of a God who does more than create. They also testify of a God who delivers, redeems, reconciles, loves, and judges. In essence, the testimony is of a God who is present in history and the events of the lives of human beings. Such testimony is both *corporate* and *individual.* Corporate testimonies of God's revealing presence are those such as the deliverance of the Jews from Egypt.

Another example, from modern times, is the affirmation of the founding fathers of the American colonies that they were led to a promised land of religious freedom. The Saints Church has, from its beginning, declared that God himself established it and continues to direct it. Deliverance from persecution has been a common thread tying the Latter Day Saints with ancient Israel.

On the individual level, numerous people with varying religious and cultural backgrounds have testified to being directed by God in both major and minor decisions in their lives. Significant numbers of people affirm that they have come to times in their lives when unexplainable occurrences have lifted them from the depths of despair. They have experienced freedom and hope and have attributed this to God's action in their lives. Such action is sometimes dramatic as in the miraculous healing of a loved one. More often God's presence is felt in small, seemingly insignificant ways. Through other people's acts of kindness and concern toward us God's love is made real in our lives. Through the prompting of his Holy Spirit we sometimes choose right over wrong. Such experiences have by no means been restricted to the so-called religious, the pious, or the deserving. On the contrary, it is frequently persons burdened by selfishness who have been granted new life by God's actions. God acts in the lives of *all* people and certainly does not discriminate. There has not been a period of history devoid of the testimony of God's action among his people. Contrary to what some say, God is not dead. He is alive and active, just as much today as in any previous era.

The term *word of God* has always been prominent in Judeo-Christian circles. In modern English the term *word* is associated with some form of written or spoken expression. In Hebrew, however, the term also applies to an *act* or *event*. Likewise in Greek, it means *action*, *deed*, or *event*. It is in this broader sense of self-expression that we understand God's *word*. Just as people express themselves by their actions, so does God. The first few verses of John's gospel use this term in reference to Jesus Christ. This is to say that Jesus Christ is the self-expression or revelation of God. Because of the importance of Christ as the central expression of God's revelation, we will take a closer look at his significance.

GOD REVEALS HIMSELF IN JESUS CHRIST

Jesus Christ is the central revelation of God. Because God is personal and it is to persons that he reveals himself, the highest expression of God is a person, who is Jesus Christ. God communicates himself to humanity most vividly through his Son. The form of a person is the highest means by which God can reveal himself because God himself is personal. Because they are persons, the form of a person is also the highest means that humans can understand. God revealed as a person is therefore the fullest, most complete revelation of God that we are capable of comprehending. In this revelation persons experience God and created humanity at the same time—God in human form.

It is difficult to acknowledge Jesus Christ as the final revelation of God if we think of him only as the historical Jesus of Nazareth. After all, we have already said that God reveals himself to all persons in all ages. Jesus Christ is seen, however, as the eternal personal expression of God, not limited to any particular time or space but ever present in all places and among all peoples.

How can this be so? Christians have experienced the presence of Christ in their lives in such a way that they have been led to confess that he is indeed alive today. The powerful testimony of the disciples who encountered Jesus on the road to Emmaeus after his crucifixion tells us that they experienced him alive even after he had been killed. That same quality of interpersonal relationship that Jesus shared with his contemporaries has been experienced by countless people through the ages since then. The expression of God in human form is certainly not confined to the historic Jesus of Nazareth. Christ is encountered daily as persons struggle to bring meaning to their lives. He lives today as God's continuing self-revelation. We do not need to rely completely on the memories of a past figure. The ever living Christ comes to us in present-day experiences.

Jesus of Nazareth was both the medium and the message of God's revelation. We cannot separate who he was from the message he taught. His message *was* his life. Jesus' spoken words were also his message but only because they were a harmonious expression of who he was. In Jesus, God confronted us with who he is in the form of a person. It is this mode of expression that makes God's revelation in Christ so important. Any additional perceptions about God that we get must be seen in the light of Jesus Christ—the central revelation. He represents the complete summation of what God can and intends to say to us about himself. Other forms of God's revelation add to our understanding of this central encounter.

The life of Jesus Christ is compelling and demands response. It is not sufficient for us to affirm that God reveals himself to us even if we know it from personal experience and believe it is true. We must ask one final question, "What difference does it make to us that God reveals himself?" This is a question of response.

THE RESPONSE TO REVELATION

When God reveals himself to us, and we recognize that we have encountered him, something happens to us. We respond in the attitudes of awe and humility. Isaiah experienced this and used the words "Woe is me" (Isaiah 6:5, I.V. and K.J.V.). We also respond by trying to interpret the revelatory experience and put it into words. In addition, we attempt to decide what meaning the revelation has for our lives and to act accordingly. These are three aspects of our response to God revealing himself to us. Although they may be complex and interrelated, we shall choose to talk about them separately.

When we are confronted by the presence of God we realize that we have been encountered by a power that is greater than we are. This solicits from us feelings of awe, dependence, thanksgiving, adoration, or praise. These are accompanied by a recognition of who we are—that our lives are dependent on something greater than our own abilities and actions. We feel humble and are forced to confess our inadequacies and dependencies. Furthermore we are overwhelmed by God's personal concern and love for us. We come to recognize that in spite of our shortcomings, God takes the initiative to reach out to us in forgiveness. We hear the call to repentance and offer our lives in response to God's call. This whole response is worship in its truest sense.

Revelatory events are of such major significance that when we are encountered by God we try to retain the essence of the experience and also to share it with others. The keeping and the sharing both require interpretation and verbalization. This is true of witnessing any major event; the principle is the same. Historians doing research frequently discover that two or more eyewitnesses to the same event relate their stories quite differently. Judges and juries in courts also have similar experiences. The reason is that people interpret happenings through the filters of their own experiences. No two persons' life experiences are identical and so no two interpretations of an event will be identical. When interpreting God's revelation, our interpretations and subsequent written or spoken statements are colored by our life experiences up to the present. It can be no other way. Our written and spoken interpretations are an important response to the revelation of God. Sometimes we think we can pass on to others the experience itself. This is, however, impossible. The best we can do is pass on our verbal interpretations of the experience. These words, whether spoken or written, are then subject to the interpretations of those who hear or read our words. These interpretations, of course, are determined by the individuals making them. Jesus tried to tell his disciples of things that he knew. In talking about the kingdom of God he used parables to capture some of the significance of what he wanted to share. The gospel account at one point indicates that Jesus said, "Whereunto shall I liken the kingdom of God? Or with what comparison shall we compare it?" (Mark 4:24, I.V.). This is true with us also. The best we can do is to say what God is *like*. Even then our expressions fall far short of capturing the essence of our experiences.

Written and spoken interpretations of revelatory experiences are, if we think of it, the "stuff" of which

Scripture is compiled. Many other interpretations of course do not become canonized however important they might be. We will consider the nature of Scripture in the next chapter. The central point here is that a very important aspect of the human response to God's revelation is interpretation and verbalizing of the experience. By sharing in this way with others, the spirit of the experience can be appreciated by persons other than those perceiving the revelation itself.

The third aspect of our response to revelation is in the meaning we decide that revelation has for our lives and the way this causes us to act. In a sense this "action" response to revelation is more important than the "verbal" response. Just as God reveals himself most effectively in actions, as persons so do we. By our actions, we reflect the influence of God in our lives. When the Holy Spirit is working within us we express the fruits of the Spirit (e.g. love, patience, kindness, etc.) in our relationships with others. Previously we referred to God's intent that human creation reflect his image. We suggested that this is one of the reasons why God reveals himself. Living in God's image is the most natural and most effective response we can make to the revelation of God. It also enables us to be instruments of his revelation of himself to others. We can at the same time live with God and with others in the spirit of his revealed presence.

CHAPTER 6

SCRIPTURE

Scripture plays a prominent part in the life of the Saints Church. A strong belief in the value of Scripture goes hand in hand with the belief in revelation discussed in the previous chapter. One of the distinctive characteristics of the Saints is that they have two other books of Scripture in addition to the Bible. These are the Book of Mormon and the Doctrine and Covenants.

Before discussing the nature of specific books of Scripture, however, we will give consideration to Scripture in general. What is Scripture and where does it come from? How do writings come to be accorded the status of Scripture? How is Scripture used by the church and by individuals? These and other questions will be addressed in this chapter.

WHAT IS SCRIPTURE?

We have talked about God's revelation of himself to his human creation and about our response to this revelation. Scripture is closely related to this response. It is the compilation of selected written interpretations of God's revelatory acts and of human responses to these acts.

It may be helpful for us to use the Bible as the source

of some examples of what comprises Scripture. The Psalms, for example, are expressions of praise stimulated by writers' realization of what God had done in the lives of individuals and of nations. The books of the prophets (e.g. Isaiah, Amos, etc.) are stories of persons who were called by God to deliver messages to the people of their day. The prophets put into words what they perceived to be the will of God for their people. The Gospels are the remembered accounts of the life and ministry of Jesus Christ. The Bible as a whole is a history of successes and failures in the continuing attempt to discover and live out God's will for people.

Writers of Scripture are not impartial objective witnesses to specific events involving other people. They are trying to express what happened *to them.* Moreover they are telling of the most significant experiences of their lives, experiences in which they have witnessed God at work. The power of the experience itself is still with the writer. We use the term *inspiration* to describe how a person writes and speaks of revelatory experience. The Scriptures are inspired writings. They reflect the efforts of those who recognize that God's Spirit is working with them as they struggle to find the best words to express what they feel and know. Scripture is the product of the Holy Spirit working within persons.

We said that Scripture is a compilation. The Bible, for example, was not written as a continuous narrative, but as many separate books. Furthermore, the compilation is a selection. Not all writings describing God's activity and subsequent human response are acknowledged as Scripture. Many are left out. How, then, is this selection accomplished?

HOW WRITINGS BECOME SCRIPTURE

As we have said the collection of sacred writings which we call Scripture plays an important part in the life of the church. These writings are a standard of belief and practice within the church. Writings which are part of the scriptural collection are included precisely because they make a contribution to what is considered to be central in the life of the church. The procedure of formally designating writings as Scripture is called *canonization*. In the history of the Christian Church this has sometimes involved long drawn-out argument and debate and at other times has been a quick, simple matter. Greater detail regarding the canonization of each of the three books of Latter Day Saint Scripture will be explored in chapters 7 and 8. Additional insight into what makes writings scriptural will be shared later in this chapter. Suffice it to say at this point that Scripture represents those selected writings which are considered to be important for the belief and practice of the church.

THE ROLE OF SCRIPTURE

Perhaps the most important questions we can ask about Scripture are questions about its value and its use in our lives. The Christian community has long claimed that Scripture has *authority*. Authority can be seen in formal, external terms. A supervisor in a place of business has authority over subordinate personnel. This authority is one which has power over individuals who are expected to obey and perform their duties within its provisions.

Authority can also be seen in an internal or informal sense. This is the authority generated by the very essence of who a person is. It is the authority which receives recognition not because obedience is commanded but because people perceive inherent values in the person exercising authority. This distinction is well illustrated in the incident of Jesus' ministry in the Sermon on the Mount. Matthew 7:29 says that "he taught them as one having authority, and not as the scribes" (K.J.V.). Jesus' authority was demonstrated in what he said and in who he was as a person rather than in any title that he had. Those who followed Jesus when he called recognized that what he said and did had meaning for their lives.

Scripture has both external and internal authority. We use and respect Scripture because the church says it is important. Years or centuries of use make it worthy of our attention. This is authority in an external sense. But there is also a sense in which each of us decides what is authoritative for us. If Scripture elicits a positive response from us—a decision to change our lives for the better—then we can say that it has authority or meaning for us. It will cause us to respond. It will make a claim on our lives. But this may not happen all at once. If a passage of scripture doesn't appeal to us at first reading its meaning may grow in our lives as exposure to it increases. For Scripture to be significant in our lives it must be consistent with our personal experience with God. Scripture is accepted by the church because it is consistent with experience over the years.

Although we said that Scripture is a response to God's revelation, it can also be a means to our own encounter with God. We are not privileged to share the *same experience* with God as did the writer of the scripture. But the scripture can lead us to experience with the *same God* as was experienced by the writer. Scripture has great power to bring us to encounter with God.

There is a sense in which Scripture is both timely and timeless. It is *timely* in that it is the account of what God is doing among people in specific places and situations. The witness of God's action is not a witness to general principles but rather to specific experiences. Furthermore, Scripture is *timeless* in that it has the capacity to communicate to persons who live in times and places far removed and who experience situations quite different from those of the writers of Scripture. Writings are chosen as Scripture precisely because they are timeless. It is possible, however, to view Scripture as so timeless that the specific situations to which Scripture is a response have been forgotten. In order to benefit from the use of Scripture today we must see it in the context of what was happening when it was written. It is only by seeing Scripture as the product of real-life situations rather than of theoretical propositions that we can use it to apply to our own situations. To use the Scriptures responsibly today we must ask not simply, "What does it say?" or even, "What did it say to the people to whom it was addressed?" Rather we must ask, "What does it say to *us today?*" For this reason we must not take the words or phrases as our guide but look behind these to the meaning.

SCHOLARSHIP AND INTERPRETATION

It is this search for the present-day meaning of Scripture that has led to what students call scriptural scholarship or *criticism*. This kind of study seeks the answers to questions about how the Scriptures were originally written, subsequently translated into modern languages, and about their meaning for us today. These inquiries can be very fruitful in clarifying what the writers were intending to say and can add insight for our present-day use of Scripture.

We are all interpreters of Scripture. There can be no such thing as "pure" Scripture. When you and I read Scripture or hear someone else read it we sift it through the filter of our own experiences, interpreting it for our own situations as we go. Knowing that all Scripture is subject to the human limitations of writer and of reader or hearer places a burden on us. We cannot simply be "at ease," absorbing the "pure" truths expressed. Instead we must continually be asking questions about Scripture's meaning for us.

Right from the time of the earliest formulations of statements of belief, Christians have affirmed that Scripture contains the Word of God. In the last chapter we introduced the meaning of the term *word of God* as God's *actions* as distinct from his *words.* Therefore to say that the Bible contains the word of God is not to claim (although some have) that in it are found God's verbal expressions. Rather it is to say that in it are found human testimonies to God's self-revealing—his Word, or action, in history.

We also said, however, that Scripture is *inspired* writing. At the same time that God reveals himself by acting in the lives of people, he also gives us the power to perceive that revelation and to interpret it. It would appear to be fruitless if God revealed himself to creatures who were unable to perceive his revelation. Inspiration is present in the writer and in the reader. Our careful exposure to Scripture can enable it to *speak* to us in the circumstances of today. Scriptural interpretation, then, is not picking and choosing those passages that appeal to us and using them to support our existing points of view. It is opening our whole selves to the claims that it makes on our lives. It is inviting the Holy Spirit into our lives and being willing to follow where God is trying to lead us.

OPEN SCRIPTURE

Scripture is open in the sense of being subject to new insights and interpretations. If we approach Scripture with an open mind and bring to it the real-life situations of which we are made up, it will speak to us. Any of us who have read selections of Scripture even a limited number of times can affirm that subsequent readings of the same passage will result in new understandings. "I had never thought of it that way before" is a familiar comment of those who read the Scriptures. Also as we attempt to determine what scriptures from a particular historical context have to say to our situation today we are opening them up to convey new meanings that persons living in the past could never have imagined.

Scripture is also open in another way. The Saints maintain that God reveals himself throughout history. In particular they testify that God reveals himself in the present. If we see Scripture as a record of God's revelatory activity and human responses over the years, then we can expect Scripture to be written in all ages. Most Christians believe the Bible to be the only authoritative Scripture. The Saints, in contrast, have insisted that the canon of Scripture includes other books. They have said that present-day writings concerning God's revelatory activity and the human response are also important. The Saints Church has three books of Scripture—the Bible, the Book of Mormon, and the Doctrine and Covenants. These three books will be explored in greater depth in chapters 7 and 8. The principle illustrated by the existence of these additional books of Scripture is that the body of Scripture can be added to as the church perceives the initiative of God among his people.

CHAPTER 7

THE BIBLE

The Bible is one of a group of Scriptures frequently referred to as the "Three Standard Books" of the Saints Church. Belief in the Bible as Scripture—as containing the word of God—is one aspect of the Saints Church which ties it to the common tradition of all Christian denominations.

It is the purpose of this chapter to give a brief overview of the content of the Bible, to look at its historical development, and to consider its use for us today. We will also discuss the "Inspired Version" of the Bible, published from manuscripts prepared by the founder of the church, Joseph Smith.

WHAT IS THE BIBLE?

The Bible has sometimes been called "the Book of the Ages." Its story covers many centuries and is the product of many cultures. The Bible is a compilation of many books written at various times in various circumstances by various people. In a sense it is a library in and of itself. The separate books, however, are not unrelated. They each bear witness to experiences where people learned something of God's will. They represent attempts to respond in words to that great revelation of God that we mentioned in Chapter 5.

The books comprising the Bible have not been hastily thrown together. They have been carefully chosen from among a large number of writings. This selection process, called *canonization*, involved considerable time and sometimes disagreement among those involved in making the decisions. The books which comprise what we call the Old Testament were finally agreed to in A.D. 90. The earliest existing list of what we now know as the New Testament books dates back to A.D. 367. The evidence shows that some books now in the Bible were barely accepted, with doubt in the minds of many as to their worthiness to be included. Other books just missed being included. Some of these are included in what is called the Apocrypha—a small collection of writings acknowledged as Scripture by the Roman Catholic Church.

Writings were chosen for inclusion in the Bible because of the value that they were felt to have in preserving a record of the religious history of people. Some were chosen because of their frequent use in worship. Others were chosen (as in the case of the first five books of the Old Testament) because for years they had been the basic law of the Israelite nation. The books were chosen because it was assumed that they would have continuing value for succeeding generations.

Writers of the books of the Bible probably had no idea that their writings would be preserved for centuries and held in high esteem by people living many years later in circumstances far different from their own. Many Old Testament books were first written after the stories had been handed down from generation to generation by ancient storytellers. What is called the *oral tradition* played a very significant role in the preservation of the history of the Israelite nation. Some New Testament books, on the other hand, existed in written form from the start and represent the work of eyewitnesses to the events described.

Methods of writing and copying were slow and primitive—especially during Old Testament times. From the time of the writing of the original manuscripts to present-day versions in many languages, there have been complex editing and translating procedures. The difficulties of translation from the language of the original texts (e.g. Hebrew and Greek) to modern English can be fully appreciated only by persons who have been involved in such translations. Another complicating factor is that in most cases the first written versions (i.e. original sources) have long been destroyed or lost. It is difficult to tell how close the earliest manuscripts that we have are to the original text. Furthermore, manuscripts, or parts of manuscripts, have been found in recent years which have turned out to be earlier, and therefore closer to the original, than the earliest manuscripts previously available. A well-known case in point is the discovery of the Dead Sea Scrolls in the 1940s. These gave scholars early manuscripts and additional information from which recent Bible translations such as *The New English Bible* have benefitted.

THE OLD TESTAMENT

The Bible is divided into two sections—the *Old Testament* and the *New Testament.* The dividing point between the two is the most important event in the history of the world as Christians see it—the birth of Jesus Christ. The Old Testament represents the history of the Jews prior to this event. It is possible to divide this first section of the Bible into several subsections.

First are the *Books of Law.* These are the first five books starting with Genesis. The Hebrews called them the *Torah.* The Law was considered of great importance by the Hebrews. These books recognize God as acting to form the Hebrew nation and leading it according to his purposes. It is in these books that the famous story of the creation is found. Also such memorable figures as Adam, Eve, Moses, Abraham, and Noah are depicted here. These first five books of the Bible are sometimes referred to as the "Books of Moses." It is fitting that they be named after him even though most scholars have concluded that he did not write all of them.

Second are the *Books of History.* Twelve books are in this group. They start with Joshua and conclude with Esther. The seven books from Joshua to II Kings are arranged in chronological order and give a history of the Israelites from their entering Canaan up to the time of their captivity in Babylon (around 586 B.C.). The books of I and II Chronicles give a second account of part of this same period. Ezra and Nehemiah pick up the story at about 536 B.C. when the Jews returned to Palestine and began to rebuild Jerusalem. Esther fits into the period 485-465 B.C.

Third are the *Books of Poetry.* There are five books in this group, beginning with Job and finishing with the Song of Solomon. Perhaps the best known is Psalms which was used by the Hebrews as their hymnal.

Fourth are the *Major Prophets.* There are five books here, beginning with Isaiah and concluding with Daniel. Each book focuses on the personality bearing its name. Prophets were recognized for the significance of the messages they brought. These prophets lived during the period of history covered by the books of history already mentioned and should be read in light of their historical settings.

Fifth are the *Minor Prophets.* There are twelve minor prophets. These are the last twelve books of the Old Testament running from Hosea to Malachi. They are not separated from the major prophets for any significant reason except that they are much shorter. All twelve together are shorter than the Book of Isaiah. The fact that they are designated "minor" should not imply that they are insignificant. Many of them carry messages of equal significance to the so-called "major" prophets.

THE NEW TESTAMENT

The New Testament contains writings related to the life and ministry of Jesus Christ and the early years of the Christian Church. These books can be arranged in three groups.

First are *The Gospels* and *Acts.* Matthew, Mark, Luke, and John are called gospels because they recount the important events in the life of Jesus. Each gospel presents a somewhat different perspective but there is much common material particularly in the three "synoptic" gospels—Matthew, Mark, and Luke. Scholars are fairly well agreed that Mark, the shortest gospel, was written first (around A.D. 70) and used as a basis for Matthew and Luke (written around A.D. 80). John was written last, around A.D. 100. Jesus is believed to have been born around 4 B.C. and he died around A.D. 30. It was not thought necessary to write a record of his ministry while he was alive, and after his death his immediate return was anticipated. It became apparent that Jesus' second coming was not to be a reality as soon as many hoped. Eyewitnesses to his life and ministry began to die, and so it was about forty years after his death that the first account was written. It has not been firmly established whether or not the gospels were written by the individuals bearing their names. In some cases (e.g. Mark) it is not even clear who these individuals were.

Acts is a continuation of Luke written by the same author. It gives an account of the early history of the Christian movement. In Acts we read of the activities of such important persons as the apostles Paul and Peter. Acts shows how Christianity grew through the power of the Holy Spirit and spread from its origin among the Jews outward to "gentile" nations. The account recognizes the struggles that the church went through as it expanded.

Second are the *Letters of Paul.* Paul, the apostle, was one of the most influential forces in the early development of Christian history. He traveled far and wide to spread the Christian gospel. He also wrote letters to the churches that he had established when he was not able to visit them personally. His letters contain significant interpretations of the Christian faith to his times. Because of the practice of adding the name of an easily recognized person to one's own writings it is almost impossible to tell for sure which books (letters) in the New Testament were in fact written by Paul. It is generally agreed that Paul wrote Romans, I and II Corinthians, Galatians, Philippians, I Thessalonians, and Philemon. It is possible that he also wrote Ephesians, Colossians, and II Thessalonians. Other persons are thought by many scholars to have written I and II Timothy and Titus. Hebrews most certainly was not written by Paul. Paul's letters are particularly significant because they were written earlier than the gospels. The first letter was written around A.D. 50.

Third are *Other Writings*. This is a miscellaneous group. The "Pastoral Epistles" (I and II Timothy and Titus) contain instructions on the duties of church officers. They are written in the manner of a pastor speaking to assistants who will succeed him. Hebrews was written to strengthen the faith of those who were tending to fall away from the fellowship into Judaic ritualism. The "general Epistles" (James, Jude, I and II Peter, and I, II, and III John) were written to all Christians rather than to local groups as in the case of Paul's letters. These seven letters are short and deal with a variety of subjects. The book of Revelation is part of a unique body of literature described as "apocalyptic." These writings involve heavy use of symbolism and admonish the reader to trust in the promises of God which will be fulfilled at the end of earthly existence. Revelation was written around A.D. 90-95 and was designed to encourage Christians who were experiencing persecution by the Romans.

THE INSPIRED VERSION

Joseph Smith, founder of the Saints Church and its leader from 1830 until his death in 1844, worked on the development of a revised version of the Bible. He began this work in 1830 after the completion of the Book of Mormon (to be discussed in the next chapter) and after the initial phases of organization of the church. He used a King James version of the Bible to mark some of the changes that he felt inspired to make. He also dictated some revisions to scribes who wrote them down. He had completed the initial work by 1833. During the remaining years of his life Joseph Smith continued to refine the text. His work was not published in his lifetime, the first edition coming off the press in 1867. Although officially titled *The Holy Scriptures*, this version is popularly known as the "Inspired Version." The title page describes it as "an inspired revision of the authorized [King James] version."

Over 90 percent of the Inspired Version is identical to the King James Version. Of the verses that include changes (2,146), more than two thirds are in the New Testament. The largest number of changes appear in Genesis, Isaiah, and the four gospels.

Some books have only minor changes and others (seven of the "minor prophets" for example) have no changes at all. The Song of Solomon is omitted entirely from the Inspired Version. Some changes are relatively insignificant in that they are changes in punctuation or the modernizing of language. (See, for example, Mark 3:2.) These rarely affect the meaning. There are, however, cases where just a few words in a verse have been changed, altering the meaning significantly. (See, for example, Matthew 4:1, 2.) In other places sizable parts of chapters have been changed or added. (See, for example, Genesis 6:26-7:76, I.V.) Throughout the revision the basic style of the King James Version is preserved in most cases, even where major changes have been made. There are places, however, where Joseph Smith modernized the language.

Although Joseph Smith did not leave a record of the basis on which he made the changes in the Bible, it is clear that he felt a strong sense of inspiration in his work. Countless persons over the years have added their personal witness to the importance of the Inspired Version in their lives. It has established itself as an authority in the life of the church. Since its publication in 1867, the Inspired Version has been maintained as the official version of the church. Some members use it exclusively, putting aside all other versions including the King James. These persons tend to view the Inspired Version as the only "complete" and "correct" version available. Increasingly, however, members use the Inspired Version along with one or more other versions, choosing that particular version which for them gives clearest expression to the chapter or verse under consideration.

USING THE BIBLE TODAY

The Bible is the best-selling book of all time. In 1971 there were 1,457 translations of at least parts of the Bible. It has been translated into virtually every known language. One modern language version sold more copies than any other book during 1972 and 1973 in the United States. It would seem that the Bible is a very popular book. But how many of the millions of copies in existence are used with any regularity? The question of appropriate use of the Bible is a complex one. We often feel that we should use the Bible more but don't know how. Should it be read from cover to cover once a year and every detail taught to our children? Of what value is it to memorize key passages? It would seem that the usefulness of the Bible needs to go beyond memorization and the accumulation of knowledge just for their own sake.

The main reason for the Bible's continuing appeal over the years is its timelessness—its ability to speak to the issues of various cultures and ages. By acquainting ourselves with the testimonies of persons in the Bible we become better equipped to handle the situations in which we find ourselves. We do not encounter identical situations to those described in the Bible. However, passages such as the parable of the Good

Samaritan (Luke 10) certainly have their present-day parallels. Its use as a guide to personal problem-solving is not the only value of the Bible. It can also help contemporary Christians see their own lives as a part of a community of believers spanning many centuries. We are not isolated in our responses to God's call in our lives. There have been millions before us who have gone through similar struggles in their efforts to respond to the same God.

The individual who wishes to become more familiar with the Bible should not be intimidated by its size or its language structure. Books should usually be read page by page starting with page one. This is not necessary with the Bible. It is composed of many books. The reader can start with any book. It may be helpful to start with the shorter books. Believe it or not, more than half of the sixty-six books can be read in an average of twenty minutes each, not one of these requiring more than an hour. A quick look at the table of contents of any Bible can direct you to these short books.

For some of us the Elizabethan English of the King James and Inspired versions is very meaningful. For others, there may be places where the archaic language acts as a barrier to understanding. This is particularly true of young people. After all, it is hardly the kind of language that we hear or use every day. Many persons prefer the modern language versions which have become readily available in recent years. In some versions the entire Bible is available. Others are available in New Testament plus certain parts of the Old Testament. With modern language versions available, archaic language need not be a barrier to our reading the Bible.

We cannot avoid developing greater familiarity

with some parts of the Bible than others. However, if we are to get maximum use from the resources contained in the Bible we need to be introduced to more of it than most of us have taken the time to read. Approaching the Bible with an open mind and a belief that it has something important to say to us will significantly enrich our lives. An understanding of how God has worked in the lives of people in the past will better enable us to perceive him working in our own lives today.

CHAPTER 8

LATTER DAY SAINT SCRIPTURES

In addition to the Bible, the Saints Church has two other books of Scripture. These are the Book of Mormon and the Doctrine and Covenants. This chapter will provide an introduction to the origin, content, and role of each.

WHAT IS THE BOOK OF MORMON AND WHERE DID IT COME FROM?

The Book of Mormon was first published in 1830, just prior to the organization of the church that same year. This book has been, from the time of its initial appearance to the present day, the subject of much speculation, attack, and subsequent defense. It was presented by the early Saints as a history of people living on the American continent from about 600 B.C. to A.D. 400. The Book of Mormon was affirmed as a translation from gold plates hidden in the ground for centuries and made available to Joseph Smith by an angel. Such claims met with feelings ranging from enthusiasm to hostility. It was also claimed that the Book of Mormon was a second witness to God's activity—a "second Bible." Even though Latter Day Saints have never maintained that the Book of Mormon replaces the Bible, the idea that there is more than one book of Scripture is still hard for most people to accept.

Very little is known about the precise way in which Joseph Smith produced the book. He did not possess language skills that would have enabled him to translate from an ancient language into modern English. It is known that he dictated the manuscript to scribes who wrote in longhand, preparing a manuscript from which the book was published. Included as part of the book are two affidavits signed by a total of eleven witnesses who affirm that they saw the plates on which the records were engraved. Other than these people, no one else claimed to have seen the plates. Contemporaries of Joseph Smith say that he remained out of sight even to the scribes while dictating. There are in existence varying descriptions of how Joseph Smith "translated." He himself simply said that it was accomplished "by the gift and power of God."

Many editions of the Book of Mormon have been printed since 1830. The most recent appeared in 1966. Small changes, mostly in grammar and punctuation, have been made over the years in attempts to communicate the message of the book more clearly.

From the outset books and pamphlets have been written and speeches delivered attempting to destroy the credibility of the book. In defense, Latter Day Saints have pursued two courses. Some members have attempted to authenticate the book by proving, through archaeological research, that the people described in the Book of Mormon did, indeed, inhabit the American continent. Decisive proof has not been forthcoming but neither has concrete evidence to the contrary. The second course of defense taken by the Saints has been to let the book speak for itself. Persons are invited to read the book to determine what meaning it has for their lives.

WHAT STORY DOES THE BOOK OF MORMON TELL?

Like the Bible, the Book of Mormon is a collection of different books with the names of different individuals attached. There are fifteen books in all, varying in length from one to thirty chapters. Fourteen of these books tell the story of a colony of people called Nephites who left Jerusalem just before its destruction in 586 B.C. The story tells of their migration to the American continent where they lived for centuries until they were destroyed by their enemies, the Lamanites, early in the fifth century. The remaining book tells of an earlier colony, the Jaredites, who migrated from the East to the West at the time of the building of the Tower of Babel.

The Book of Mormon can be divided into parts as follows:

1. *I and II Nephi.* These books were written by Nephi, the leader of the colony that left Jerusalem, crossed the ocean, and settled in America. They tell the story of the migration.
2. *Jacob.* This book was written by Jacob and continues the record of his brother, Nephi.
3. *Enos, Jarom, and Omni.* These are all very short books continuing the religious history of the people.
4. *Words of Mormon.* This is a short insertion added by Mormon who prepared the records for preservation in a hill before he died.
5. *Mosiah, Alma, and Helaman.* These three books represent about half of the total Book of Mormon. They give accounts from the religious and civil life of the people covering almost two centuries.

6. *III and IV Nephi.* These two books recount the visitation and ministry of Jesus Christ to the Western world. They also tell of a period of harmony followed by division into two conflicting groups.

7. *Mormon.* This book tells of the end of the Nephites, climaxing in the closing battle between the two groups. Mormon assembled all the previous records and abridged them into one account.

8. *Ether.* This book tells the story of the earlier people, the Jaredites, originally written by their prophet, Ether. It was abridged by Moroni, the son of Mormon.

9. *Moroni.* This book was written by Moroni, the lone survivor of the Nephites. He completed the record and buried the plates.

As a whole, the Book of Mormon contains historical narrative interspersed with spiritual admonition. The style is similar in many ways to the King James version of the Bible.

HOW IS THE BOOK OF MORMON USED TODAY?

In the years immediately after its publication the Book of Mormon was the primary missionary tool of the infant church. Representatives of the church traveled great distances sharing the Book of Mormon with anyone who would hear them. This book, above any other single thing, was responsible for the way both supporters and opponents viewed the young church. In fact, early Latter Day Saints were called Mormons after the title of this new book of Scripture.

From the early years of the church up to the present day there have been a number of different ways in which Latter Day Saints view the Book of Mormon.

First, it is viewed as evidence that God reveals

himself in all ages and that the written response to that revelation is important enough to be given the status of Scripture.

Second, it is viewed as an additional witness to Jesus Christ. The Book of Mormon includes an account of Jesus' ministry among the people of the American continent.

Third, it is viewed as supplementing the Bible's collection of testimony relating to God acting in the lives of his people.

Fourth, it is viewed as an authentic history of American Indian ancestors. As such, the book is considered of particular value by members who have contacts with Indian people.

No one of these views is necessarily more significant than others. They have all been present with varying degrees of emphasis throughout the history of the church. Individual members may consider all, some, or none of these views to reflect their personal understanding of the Book of Mormon.

Like the Bible, the Book of Mormon is read from the pulpit in public worship. It is also used by members in their individual and family devotional lives. In addition, it has been a popular subject of study in church school settings. The Book of Mormon is not intended to replace the Bible. It is designed to stand beside it, being *in addition to* rather than instead of the Bible. It is a matter of individual preference as to which book is used more frequently. Some members use the Book of Mormon more than the Bible, others less. Most members allow both to speak to their life situations.

Throughout the years since its publication, the Book of Mormon has been one of the distinctive resources and identifying characteristics of the Saints Church.

Thousands of members bear powerful testimony of its influence in their lives. All persons are invited to read the book so that they can form their own opinions about its value.

WHAT IS THE DOCTRINE AND COVENANTS AND WHAT DOES IT CONTAIN?

The Doctrine and Covenants is a compilation of documents that the church accepts as representing "the mind and will of God" and as a standard of church law and practice. The documents date back to 1828 and cover the period from then until the present. With a few exceptions, each section of the book was authored by one of the five presidents of the church. One of the specific functions of the president (or *prophet* as he is also called) is to present in written form what he considers to be God's will for the church. The documents are presented to the various councils and quorums of the church (see Chapter 11) and to the World Conference for their consideration. After a formal vote, sections are printed as additions to the Doctrine and Covenants.

Early in the life of the church the documents, or "revelations" as they are commonly called, were printed in the church periodical. In 1835 they were published in book form as the Doctrine and Covenants. Many editions have appeared over the years with additional sections being added. By 1974, the book consisted of 151 sections. The first 113 of these were written between the years 1828 and 1844, most of them by Joseph Smith. Sections 114 through 131 were written during the presidency of the founder's son, Joseph Smith III (1860-1914), and all but one were authored by him. Sections 132 through 138 were written by Frederick M. Smith, third president of the church, during the years 1914-1946. Sections 139-144 were written by Israel A. Smith, fourth president during the years 1946-1958. Sections 145-151 were written between 1958 and 1974 by W. Wallace Smith. The Saints expect that additional sections will be added in the future.

The sections of the Doctrine and Covenants include several different kinds of material. The early sections of the book, presented by Joseph Smith, contain much personal instruction directed to individuals who were prominent in the church at the time. These same sections are also concerned to a large extent with details of church government and organization. Other matters of major significance that were addressed in early sections are Zion (see Chapter 14) and stewardship (see Chapter 16). It is understandable why such a large proportion of the content of the Doctrine and Covenants originated during the first four years of the church's life (1830-1833). The church needed clarification regarding basic principles of doctrine and organization.

Sections of the Doctrine and Covenants added after 1860 have nearly all been presented in answer to specific concerns or problems. Most of the recent documents begin with the designation of persons to serve in the leading quorums of the church and then follow with counsel and admonition to the church at large.

Although there are differences in style and phraseology among the documents presented by the five presidents of the church, we are able to identify a basic similarity. As we have said before, the prophet has the responsibility to present to the church written expressions of what he feels to be God's will for the church. It has become traditional to follow the basic style adopted by Joseph Smith who frequently expressed himself in the first person, attributing the statements to God or Jesus Christ. This style tends to add authority to what is being said. Unfortunately the first person language and the designation of the sections of the Doctrine and Covenants as "revelations" have led some members of the church to claim infallibility for the words themselves. It is appropriate, instead, to consider the sections of the Doctrine and Covenants to be the inspired interpretation of revelatory experience by the prophet of the church.

Many sections of the Doctrine and Covenants contain words and phrases reminiscent of the Elizabethan English characteristic of the Bible, particularly the King James version, and also of the Book of Mormon. The frequency with which this style is used varies from one president of the church to another, decreasing in recent years.

USING THE DOCTRINE AND COVENANTS TODAY

From its first printing in 1835, the Doctrine and Covenants has been used as the basic authority on church practice and organization. In it are contained descriptions of the various priesthood offices and the methods for administering the ordinances (see Chapter 10). This is one of its most important uses even today.

Like the Book of Mormon, it is also viewed as evidence that God still reveals himself and that the canon of Scripture is open. Furthermore, those parts of the Doctrine and Covenants which provide admonition, doctrinal statements, etc., are used in public worship. These parts are also used in individual and family worship. The book as a whole is a popular resource for church school study, especially by adults.

As is true for the Bible and Book of Mormon, the Doctrine and Covenants is both timely and timeless. The various sections of the book were addressed to particular historical situations and in some cases to one or a few particular persons. It is helpful for us to read what is said to other people at other times. If we do this, however, we must pay close attention to the circumstances in which the statements were presented. This is of course more true of a statement to an individual than it is of something describing procedure or organization. Nevertheless, careful consideration of the historical context of each section is necessary if it is to be fully understood. Scripture really cannot be used effectively today unless we consider both the similarities and the differences between the circumstances in which it was written and those in which we live. There is a sense in which the scripture has to be reinterpreted for our day if it is to be helpful to us in meeting our day-to-day situations.

The relationship between the Doctrine and Covenants and the Bible and Book of Mormon is similar to the previously described relationship between the Bible and Book of Mormon. All three books complement each other and each has its particular value. They all affirm Jesus Christ as the central element of the gospel. Their joint witness to God's activity among the people of all ages has the power to support us in our individual and corporate endeavors to follow Christ. Members of the Saints Church are justly proud of their two unique books of Scripture. They invite others to become familiar with what these books have to say.

CHAPTER 9

THE NATURE AND PURPOSE OF THE CHURCH

The church means many things to many people. To some it is a group of people. To others it is a building. To still others it is a set of beliefs or style of behavior. All these and others are integral parts of what we call the church. The church is a multifaceted and complex entity. In this chapter we will take a look at some of the ways in which the Saints Church sees itself and ways that others see it. We will address the question, "What is the church?" We will also examine some of the major ingredients that comprise the church. We will look at its life and consider its purpose.

It is true that the church is buildings, beliefs, and behavior. But above all it is people. People constitute the heart of the church. The church is not just any people, however. It is those who have taken upon themselves the name of Jesus Christ. It is those who acknowledge that God is creator and sustainer of the universe and that he is their Lord. The church is a community of people endeavoring to bear witness of these realities to a world which is not conscious of them. It is those who have covenanted with God to work with him to accomplish his purposes. The church is, on the one hand, the entire body of believers. Yet it is possible to refer to a particular denomination such as the Saints Church as the church also.

CALLING AND PURPOSE

From the time of its organization, the Saints Church has affirmed that it was brought into existence by God to fulfill his purposes. The Saints claim to be a chosen people. But, we must ask, chosen for what? The Hebrew people understood themselves to be chosen. They thought at first that this meant that they were to receive special favors. But with the passage of time and years of struggle they came to realize that there was more to being chosen than receiving. They came to understand that they were called to do something—that being chosen is more a matter of giving than receiving. Likewise the Saints see themselves as called for a purpose. They are called and chosen to bring the reality of the love of God into the lives of people. They believe they are chosen to establish God's kingdom here in this world by bringing their unique resources to bear in the places where they live.

While affirming that they are a chosen people the Saints avoid claiming that they are the only people that are chosen to fulfill God's purposes in the world. The Saints recognize that they are one of many groups of persons witnessing for Christ. However, they find meaning and purpose in that particular identity which is uniquely theirs.

Many times throughout the history of Christianity the church has been called the *body of Christ*. This term has significant meaning and can help us better understand the nature of the church. To say that the church is the body of Christ means that it is God's living presence on earth just as Jesus was centuries ago. It means that the church is called to do God's work in his world just as Jesus did. The image of the "body" has additional meaning, too. A body is a unified whole, yet it consists of different parts with each performing its own functions. So it is with the church. In the deepest sense the Saints Church shares a profound heritage with the larger Christian community or body. Yet it affirms its own unique experience of calling and authority and has its own life as a body of believers.

In the larger sense, the church encompasses all those past, present, and future who recognize Jesus as Lord. In a narrower sense, the church refers to those who at a point in time hold membership in the Reorganized Church of Jesus Christ of Latter Day Saints. It is important that when dwelling on one of these two views of the church we remember the other. Whichever view we are emphasizing at a given time, the people who comprise the church are the main ingredients. We have said that they are people with a purpose, a calling, and a mission. They have been chosen for a task. On the way to accomplishing this task they involve themselves in many activities. The life of the members, the resources that they bring, and the activities in which they engage are all important aspects of what we call the church. These are what make the community of people "the church" rather than just another group of people.

The gospel of Jesus Christ does not exist in a vacuum nor is it communicated primarily by the written or spoken word. Earlier in this book we emphasized how God's word is a word of action that is communicated through personal relationship, particularly in the life and ministry of Jesus Christ. In the same way the life of the church is characterized by action, by doing. The life-style of the church and its members is one of tangible expression of the essence of God as he was revealed in Jesus Christ. As the body of Christ, the church is constantly active and on the move.

In maintaining faithfulness to its calling, the church is sustained by the power of the Holy Spirit. This living presence of God has kept the Christian Church alive from the first century. Like all organizations, the church sometimes loses sight of its purpose. It becomes distracted by outside influences that appear to overwhelm it. The church also becomes ingrown, self-centered, and bent on its own survival. If it were not for God's continued presence through his Holy Spirit the church would have died long ago. The Holy Spirit provides a corrective influence that helps to keep the church centered on its mission. Because of our God-given freedom to choose, however, the influence of the Holy Spirit is sometimes ignored by human beings who make up the church.

As the church attempts to fulfill its purpose it tries first to discover where God is active in the world bringing about his purposes. Jesus said he came to "preach deliverance to the captives, and recovering of sight to the blind; to set at liberty them that are bruised" (Luke 4:18, I.V. and KJV). Because the church is the body of Christ, it acquaints itself with the world around it so that it becomes aware of the "captives," the "blind," and the "bruised." The church cannot act for God unless it knows where God is acting and where his people are in need. The church goes further. It witnesses to the unbeliever of what God has done for humanity. It brings his redeeming word to all who will listen. It tells the good news.

Furthermore, the church identifies itself closely with those in need as it participates with God in his work in the world. Jesus resisted the temptation to completely remove himself from the ills of the world. He immersed himself in its needs. He gave himself fully. He gave his life, not just by dying on the cross but by giving of his living moments so that others might have new life. In being the body of Christ the church likewise gives its life and resists the temptation to be preoccupied with institutional self-preservation and status.

THE CHURCH GATHERS AND SCATTERS

The church is a community of people that gathers in God's name and then goes out in his name. The church gathers together frequently, usually in church buildings. This is so that the members can share common interests and maintain a sense of identity and community. Gathering together also serves an *enabling* function. It provides the members with the necessary power and strength to do God's will. In gathering, the church involves itself in four functions: worship, education, pastoral care, and stewardship. The *worship* life of the church provides for corporate expression of our recognition of God as creator and sustainer. It also permits us to see ourselves for who we are in light of the majesty of God and to hear his word of love and acceptance. Worship also solicits from us our offering of ourselves and our resources to his work in response to what he has done for us. Through *education* the members of the church learn about the heritage of the church and come to a greater understanding of its mission. Education also helps the church understand and appreciate the world into which it is sent on God's behalf. In *pastoral care* the church expresses the caring, reconciling love of God among its members. It develops a sense of unity while preserving the uniqueness of each individual member. By exercising responsible *stewardship* the church reflects the priorities laid on it by its purpose. The resources of the church are used in ways that are faithful to the purpose of God, the interests of its members, and the needs of the communities in which it is located.

The church does more than equip and enable its members through these gathered ministries. It also goes out into the world at God's direction. The church witnesses of the gospel through the process of *evangelism.* It gives of itself by reaching out to those who have not experienced God's love. It is through this process of evangelism that *Zion building* is accomplished. The church acts as the agent of transformation of the societies of the world into the kingdom of God.

More will be said about these functions in later chapters. It is important to note here that both *gathered* and *scattered* aspects of the church are vital to its task and life. The church that gathers but never goes out becomes ingrown and self-centered, never coming in contact with the world to which God has sent it and in which he is working out his purposes. On the other hand the church that scatters into the world and never gathers together becomes out of touch with its Lord and lost in the evils of the world which he wants it to overcome. The church struggles continually to keep these two integral elements of its life in appropriate balance.

GOALS AND OBJECTIVES

We live in rapidly changing times. One person has said that the only certain thing is that things will change. It is necessary, therefore, that the church continually examine its mission, priorities, and goals. The *basic* call of the church to be God's witness to the world remains unchanged. But the changing nature of the world to which it is sent demands that the church constantly take new looks at how this responsibility is carried out. In 1964, President W. Wallace Smith presented this counsel to the church:

> Instruction which has been given in former years is applicable in principle to the needs of today and should be so regarded by those who are seeking ways to accomplish the will of their heavenly Father. But the demands of a growing church require that these principles shall be evaluated and subjected to further interpretation.—Doctrine and Covenants 147:7.

These words came at a time when the church was beginning a soul-searching look at its purpose and mission in view of a rapidly changing world. In 1966 the church adopted six objectives to guide its operation in subsequent years. These were refined and restated in 1973 and read as follows:

1. *Theological Task.* Increase our understanding of the meaning of the gospel of Jesus Christ and enable each person to be faithful in relationships with God and other persons.
2. *Worth of Persons.* Emphasize the ultimate value of persons and provide the environment in which the entire range of human relationship is enriched.
3. *A World Church.* Deepen the dimensions of the World Church through the mutual sharing of cultural experience and resources.
4. *Corporate Life.* Enrich the corporate life of the church.
5. *Evangelistic Life.* Develop concepts and procedures for deepening the evangelistic life of the church.
6. *Zion.* Interpret the Zionic concept for our day in world terms and pursue the implementation of Zionic development.

Of necessity these objectives are general. Their implementation by way of specific program is worked out individually by the local jurisdictions of the church. To aid local program development, resources are produced by offices at the church headquarters. These six objectives will need to be refined and updated as circumstances change.

RESTORATION

Keeping faithful to its mission is one of the important challenges which continually confront the church. The Saints Church was born in a period of American history in which concern over the condition of the Christian Church and its various denominations was prominent. There was emphasis on the restoration of the church. Restoration differs from reformation. *Reformation* means to make necessary changes in order to remove faults and abuses and return something to a former good state. *Restoration* means to bring back something that existed formerly but has since been lost. The Saints Church originated as part of what is termed the Restoration movement in American religious history. At this time many people felt that the churches of the day were in a state of serious decay and had lost their ability to be God's agents in the world. Emphasis was on the way in which God was acting in history to restore his church. Many new churches were formed during this period.

At times the Saints have been preoccupied with what specific aspects of church organization and procedure were restored at particular times. Restoration has sometimes been seen as one or more *events*. The concept has broader meaning, however. It is possible to identify a restoration *principle*. By this we mean bringing back the church's faithfulness and vitality to its mission. This process is continual. It never ceases. Attempts to restore the church to its calling are continually being made. But, we may ask, why is restoration necessary?

The need for restoration presupposes a falling away or what is sometimes called *apostasy.* It is possible to see apostasy, as some see restoration, as an event that happened at a particular point in time. But this concept also has broader meaning. We can identify a process of apostasy. It is the tendency of the church to lose sight of its true purpose and meaning and subsequently lose its effectiveness as God's agent in the world. Apostasy takes many forms. At times the church may be so locked in to traditional patterns that it is not sufficiently flexible to meet the demands of a changing world. At other times the church may be so overanxious to accommodate itself to the trends of existing cultures that it loses sight of its mission to be the people of God. At still other times the church may simply become overwhelmed by the magnitude of its calling and resort to carrying on business as usual without accomplishing anything significant. All these are evidences of apostasy and therefore of the need for restoration.

THE CALL TO UNITY

The life of the church evidences a continual struggle against internal and external forces which lead it astray. Being the church in the present day is a call to unity and purpose. *Unity* within the church does not mean that all members think and act alike. Unity means that all accept the unique contributions of each other and work toward the common purpose for which God called the church into existence. A vital ingredient of church unity is *trust.* For the church to accomplish its purpose each member must trust the others. We must trust others to use their individual resources, experiences, and interests to make their contributions to God's work in the best way that they see fit. We are each unique persons. As such our beliefs, attitudes, and actions will vary. The church allows room for this pluralism. Unity and diversity can coexist in the church if unity is seen as dedication to the same goals and diversity is seen as a variety of ways of achieving these goals.

The third objective that we stated above was that of being a world church. The Saints Church has membership in thirty countries on all five continents. Thirteen of these countries have become bases of operation of the church since 1960. This recent period has been one in which the church has attempted to establish itself in various cultures in ways that permit indigenous expressions of the Christian gospel. Practices vary among these cultures, yet the worldwide church retains an important sense of unity. All persons, regardless of their cultural surroundings, work toward the common goal of being God's presence in the world.

A COVENANT PEOPLE

Being a member of the church implies existence in a state of covenant. A *covenant* is an association between two parties. God is the initiator of the covenant as he gives himself in love to all people. This is a gift in the truest sense. There are no strings attached. It is freely given to *everyone*. We are the receivers of the covenant and are invited to respond. Our response through wisely using what we have strengthens and fulfills the covenant. To be a member of the church is to respond by entering into the covenant relationship offered by God. This is the meaning of the initiatory ordinance of baptism. In this event persons present themselves to covenant with God. They accept the responsibility to witness of God's love and to assist in his work. Membership in the church means being one of a community of persons dedicated to the task of being God's presence in his world. The Saints extend the invitation to membership to all persons, encouraging them to join God's people in responding to his call.

CHAPTER 10

ALL ARE CALLED

In 1887, Joseph Smith III, second president and son of the founder of the Saints Church, said, "All are called according to the gifts of God unto them" (Doctrine and Covenants 119:8b). This principle is central to the life of the church. In this chapter we will begin to look at the life of the Saints Church in greater depth than was possible in the previous chapter. We will consider the responsibilities of all members as they function within the church, working together to accomplish its purpose. Various functions and roles assumed by different individuals will be examined. Brief descriptions of the sacraments of the church will also be given.

THE CALLING OF EVERY MEMBER

The Saints have always stressed the importance of the worthful contribution of each member to the church's life. The image of the church as the body of Christ has meaning here. The first century Apostle Paul originated the use of this image as indicated in I Corinthians 12. He says that *all* members of the body are necessary for the full and effective functioning of the whole. If one member is sick or lazy then the whole body is rendered less effective.

Because no two of us are identical in interests and abilities, we will each find different ways to express ourselves in response to God's call. No particular role, function, or responsibility is more or less important than the others. All are of equal value and importance and are equally acceptable to God. The image of the body is illustrative of this principle. A seemingly small disfunction of the physical body can incapacitate a person for a long time. On the other hand, our continued well-being is maintained by tiny organs that we scarcely know exist.

Concern over whether one function is more important than another usually arises when calling is seen in terms of status, power, and reward. When being chosen (or called) is seen in terms of obligation, responsibility, and service, however, one is humbled by the magnitude of the task. To be a member of the church is primarily a call to serve. This is depicted by Jesus' attitude of humility as he washed his disciples' feet (John 13:5-16). His parable regarding persons who were invited to a wedding (Luke 14:8-11) cautions us against asserting our own importance. Regardless of the particular role that we might play in the church, our primary calling is to be members of the body of Christ along with all other members.

CALLED TO PARTICULAR RESPONSIBILITIES

In addition to the general obligations of discipleship accepted by each one, members of the Saints Church have particular responsibilities. Except in rare cases, there is *not* a single, full-time minister appointed to care for the various needs of the local church. Instead the responsibilities for presiding, preaching, scripture reading, ministry to the sick, visiting in homes, etc., are shared by a number of individuals. Members of the local church also share such functions as church school teaching, youth group leadership, and maintenance services.

This structure of shared responsibility has the advantage of involving a large number of the members in various functions of the church. On the other hand, there is always a shortage of well-equipped volunteers. Few of the members have had opportunity for formal education or training in the fields in which they serve. This is especially true of such important functions as preaching and worship leadership. However, tradition and practice have supported the view that the system used by the Saints has merit and is workable.

In 1832, Joseph Smith counseled church members to "seek ye out of the best books words of wisdom; seek learning even by study, and also by faith" (Doctrine and Covenants 85:36a). Local church personnel are encouraged to raise their levels of expertise so that they can better meet the needs of the church. An important example of this was the founding by the church of Graceland College in 1895 which still functions as a liberal arts college. Correspondence courses on various church-related subjects are available from the church headquarters. In the 1970s emphasis on education is evident with the formation of the Temple School of Zion. Local, regional, and national workshops, institutes, and seminars are planned with the intent to assist members as they serve the church in their home areas. Members are also encouraged to take advantage of educational opportunities in their communities.

THE CONCEPT AND OFFICES OF PRIESTHOOD

By sharing the various responsibilities of church life among a number of people, the task of ministry is decentralized. In recognition of the diversity of gifts and interests among persons, some are ordained to specific responsibilities. The term priesthood is used to refer to these functions of ministry in the Saints Church. Ordination in the Saints Church grants specific rights and responsibilities to those on whom it is bestowed. Those who are ordained hold office in either the *Aaronic priesthood* or the *Melchisedec priesthood.* The Aaronic priesthood is named after Aaron who was consecrated by Moses to the priest's office (see Leviticus 8). The Melchisedec priesthood is named after Melchisedec, a great high priest of Old Testament times (see Psalm 110:4 and Hebrews 5:6, 10).

Within the Aaronic priesthood are the offices of deacon, teacher, and priest. *Deacons* have major responsibilities for the physical well-being of the members. They prepare and maintain the church buildings for the use of the people. They also usher persons to their seats and collect offerings during worship services. The *teachers'* ministry is mainly with individuals in counseling them on various matters as needs arise. Their primary concern is for reconciliation and harmonious relationships among members. *Priests* have major responsibilities in home ministry programs where they make regular visits to members' homes to assure them of the church's concern for them. They may also preach and perform certain sacraments of the church. Members of the Aaronic priesthood may perform certain other duties in the absence of members of the Melchisedec priesthood.

The Melchisedec priesthood contains two subdivisions, the elder and the high priest. Both of these offices have specialized functions within them. *Elders* are responsible for administrative work such as presiding over local church units (branches, congregations, missions, or groups). They also preside over worship services, preach, and administer all of the sacraments of the church. Certain elders who function in evangelistic ministries, particularly where there is opportunity to share the church's message with nonmembers, are ordained to the office of *seventy*.

High priests have the responsibility of presiding over large branches and congregations and over districts, stakes, and regions of the church. They also administer the sacraments of the church. Within the overall category of high priestly ministry are several specialized functions. *Bishops* have responsibility for the financial affairs of the church at all levels. They also coordinate the work and training of members of the Aaronic priesthood. *Evangelists* (or *patriarchs* as they are sometimes called) are primarily involved in revival and patriarchal ministries. *Apostles* supervise the work of the church in the countries where it is organized and may, when occasion requires, administer the various divisions of the headquarters structure. They are the chief missionaries of the church throughout the world and constitute a second presidency for the entire church.

The president of the church and his two counselors constitute the quorum of the *First Presidency* which presides over the high priesthood (all high priests, including bishops, evangelists, and apostles) and over the whole church. The president of the Saints Church also has the responsibility for presenting inspired counsel and instruction to the church. Documents that he presents in the course of fulfilling this function are, following approval by legislative process, included in the Doctrine and Covenants. W. Wallace Smith who is now serving as president of the church was preceded in this office by two of his brothers, Israel A. Smith and Frederick M. Smith, by his father, Joseph Smith III, and by his grandfather, Joseph Smith, Jr.

Persons holding the various priesthood offices are organized into quorums, orders, and councils. Separate groupings are established for each office. Quorum organization is for the purposes of orientation to duties, instruction to bring about improved performance, and other matters.

It is important to add that many functions in church life are performed by persons holding offices other than those for which these functions are their specific responsibility. Who does what varies from one local situation to another. Many local units of the Saints Church are very small with less than fifty active members. In such cases there may be only two or three priesthood members. The largest congregation of the church has 2,000 members on its rolls with several hundred in the priesthood. In the larger units, opportunity is given for priesthood members to perform those functions specified by their various offices. In smaller units, priesthood members may function in a number of areas. For example, in smaller congregations members of the Aaronic priesthood frequently preach sermons and preside over worship services. This rarely happens in larger groups where sufficient members of the Melchisedec priesthood are available to do this.

Although the Saints Church has always insisted that there is no ranking or hierarchy of priesthood, persons are often called from one office to another. Individuals who hold priesthood are usually first called to one or more of the three offices of the Aaronic priesthood. Many are later ordained to the office of elder. Some elders are later called to function as seventies or high priests. In the majority of local units of the church deacons, teachers, priests, and elders are found. In the larger units high priests, bishops, seventies, and evangelists also serve. Many individuals serve all their adult lives in one office while others hold several over a period of years. There is no minimum or maximum number of years that a person may occupy any particular office. Ordination is not usually granted to persons under the age of sixteen, and many receive their first call during their adult years.

Priesthood members are called to specific offices by church officials responding to the spirit of inspiration and discernment. In local situations the presiding officer presents a name with specific office to the next highest officer for consideration. After all appropriate authorities have approved, the candidate is asked to accept the call. If it is accepted, the call is presented to the members in the local area where the candidate lives for their approval. If approval is received, the candidate is then ordained and given a certificate of ordination.

The two major criteria for calling a person to the priesthood are the gifts which the person has developed and the need for persons to function in certain responsibilities. Presiding officers keep these two criteria in mind as they prayerfully seek to determine which persons should be called to which offices. Up to this time, ordination to the priesthood of the Saints Church has been conferred only on men.

Although, traditionally, ordained persons have held most of the leadership roles in the Saints Church, unordained persons may frequently be found performing various functions usually carried out by members of the priesthood. In recent years there has developed a greater openness to the use of unordained persons in leadership roles and in the decision-making process.

THE SACRAMENTS OF THE CHURCH

One important area of the resonsibilities of priesthood is the administering of the sacraments of the church. Sacraments have always been central to the lives of those who are seeking to follow Christ. A sacrament is a religious act, ceremony, or practice in which symbols are used to signify the covenant relationship between God and his human creation. Sacraments have always played a prominent role in the public worship of the Saints Church. We shall now take a brief look at each of the sacraments celebrated by the church.

Baptism is the celebration of God's gift of grace to humanity and the response of the individual in commitment to him. It is the rite of initiation into the church. Persons are eligible for baptism when they reach the age of eight, sometimes called the "age of accountability." Baptism is usually preceded by formal or informal instruction of the candidate regarding some of the basics of church history, doctrine, and practice. The prerequisites for admission to the church through baptism are the demonstration of a spirit of repentance and a desire to follow Christ to the best of one's ability. Persons who request baptism usually feel that they can best serve Christ through association with members of the Saints Church. Baptism is by immersion in water and is performed by a priest, elder, or high priest in the church. Most church sanctuaries include a baptismal font and the celebration of this sacrament is witnessed by the members in a worship setting.

Confirmation represents the response of God to the

one who has been baptized. It acknowledges in the baptized person thc gift of the Holy Spirit and is sometimes called "baptism of the Spirit." It represents the completion of the initiatory rite and admission to full membership in the church. Confirmation is performed by elders or high priests who lay their hands on the head of the seated candidate while one of them offers the prayer of confirmation. Confirmation sometimes occurs at the same service of worship as the baptism. Preferably, a space of a few days or weeks is allowed to elapse.

Blessing of children is patterned after the gospel accounts of Jesus receiving and touching children in the Bible (see Mark 10:13-16 [10:11-14, IV] and the Book of Mormon (see III Nephi 8:23). This sacrament recognizes the gift of new birth into the world. The parents and members of the church acknowledge the new life and accept responsibility for its nurture. Blessing usually occurs when a baby is a few weeks or months old but children beyond this age may also be blessed. The infant is brought to elders or high priests who hold the child while one of them offers the prayer of blessing.

The Lord's Supper is usually celebrated at the regular morning worship service on the first Sunday of each month. This is custom; however it is also celebrated at other times when appropriate. The form of this sacrament is indicated in Doctrine and Covenants 17:22, 23. The essentials are that the members of the church kneel while specified prayers are read, one over the bread and one over the wine, by priests, elders, or high priests. These priesthood members then serve the emblems to the assembled members. The most common procedure is for individual portions of bread and glasses of unfermented grape juice to be prepared ahead of the service. The congregation then kneels while the prayer of blessing is offered on the bread. Next the bread is served by the priesthood to the congregation which is seated. Then the congregation kneels again for the prayer of blessing on the wine after which the wine is served. Variations of this procedure find the use of whole loaves which are broken during the service, members coming from their seats to the front of the church to be served, etc.

The Saints Church has traditionally adopted a stance of close communion. This means that the emblems are served to baptized members of the Saints Church only. The Lord's Supper is in one sense a reaffirmation of the pledge made at baptism. It therefore has special significance for those who have been baptized into the particular fellowship of the Saints Church. The Lord's Supper is also an act of joyous thanksgiving for God's acts of redemption. In addition, this sacrament is an affirmation and renewal of the fellowship of the believer with Christ and with the church.

Marriage is an important sacrament in the Saints Church. Priests, elders, and high priests have legal and religious authority to perform marriages. Marriage signifies a bond of commitment between two persons. It acknowledges their individuality and also their oneness. It is usually celebrated in a public worship setting where the couple's friends and relatives can witness their commitment. In recent times, wedding ceremonies have become much more varied but still center on the vows establishing the covenant relationship (see Doctrine and Covenants 111:2).

Administration to the sick is available on request to persons whether or not they are members of the Saints

Church. Persons who are experiencing physical, mental, or other forms of suffering are invited to call for elders or high priests to administer to them. Administration takes the form of anointing a person's head with specially consecrated olive oil and offering a prayer to God for that person's welfare. The priesthood members lay their hands on the person's head while the prayer is offered. Administration usually occurs at a person's bedside at home or in a hospital with few if any friends or relatives present. However, it is sometimes made a part of a worship service.

This procedure has sometimes been called "healing" after the practice of Jesus and his disciples. The Saints are, however, careful to point out that God alone can heal a person. For this reason it is not wise or possible to predict what may or may not happen following administration. Whatever the outcome may be, persons have the opportunity to affirm the sovereignty of God and be thankful for whatever blessings they experience. Moreover, administration should never be seen as a replacement for services of the medical profession. The Saints believe that God works through the developed talents of persons in restoring his children to health. Administration is a demonstration that God cares and that his children have faith in his power.

Ordination of persons to the priesthood and the designating of some for specific responsibility is also accomplished by the laying on of hands. Ordination to the office of high priest is performed by high priests, to the office of elder by elders or high priests, and to the offices of the Aaronic priesthood by priests, elders, or high priests. Ordination prayers are spoken and the procedure usually occurs in a public worship setting.

Patriarchal blessings are prayers offered by evangelists-patriarchs using the laying on of hands. Individuals above the age of about sixteen may request a patriarchal blessing. Usually only one blessing is given to each individual and is usually requested at a turning point in the individual's life. The occasion of graduation from high school and beginning of college or full-time employment is the time when many blessings are given. The prayer of blessing is a request for wisdom and guidance throughout the person's life. Blessings are usually given in the privacy of a home or office with only the patriarch and the individual requesting the blessing present. The prayers of blessing are recorded or written in shorthand and then typed up so that the individual concerned can keep a copy. It is a lifelong blessing and is referred to often over the years of one's life.

The sacraments have always been a vital element in the life of the church. They provide opportunity for members to see their own individual covenants in the light of the whole church community which is called to be the body of Christ. *All* persons are called to participate in God's work. Even though some persons are asked to accept specific responsibilities, the *primary* calling of all is to be disciples of Jesus Christ. The members of the Saints Church extend this invitation and make this possibility available to all.

CHAPTER 11

CHURCH ORGANIZATION

This chapter will provide an overview of the official functions carried on within the church. There are various levels of organization in the church in which administrative, legislative, and judicial processes occur. A brief overview of these levels of organization and these functions will be presented.

CHURCH ADMINISTRATION

The First Presidency, composed of the president and two counselors, presides over all affairs of the church. The three members function as a quorum in such a way that the decisions of any one member are considered to be the decisions of the First Presidency as a quorum. Consultation among the three members occurs frequently. Supervision of the work of the church is divided among the members of this quorum so that the affairs of the church can be administered most effectively. The six major areas supervised by the First Presidency are field ministries, financial services, administrative services, program services, program planning, and patriarchal ministry (see Chart A, p. 116).

FIELD MINISTRIES: It is the current practice for the president of the Council of Twelve Apostles to serve as Director of Field Ministries. This is by assignment of the First Presidency. As president of his own quorum he has inherent responsibility for the leadership of the Twelve in their quorum functions and responsibilities. He supervises the administrative line of the church through other apostles to whom the various regions, stakes, national missions, and unorganized areas are assigned. Chart B, p. 117, presents a basic outline of field organization. Within the United States and Canada, both stake and regional patterns of organization are found.

Stakes are organized in areas (usually metropolitan) where there exist fairly high concentrations of members. As of 1975, there were seventeen stakes in the church ranging in membership from two thousand to nine thousand each. The largest concentration is in the Kansas City metropolitan area where over twenty thousand reside in four stakes. Within each stake there are between ten and twenty congregations and missions. A *congregation* will usually have its own

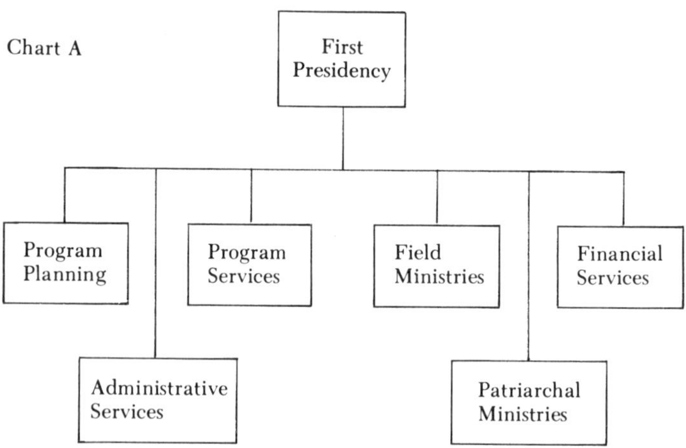

building and program of activities. However, in stake organization emphasis is placed on coordinated program and shared facilities between the various congregations. *Missions* are units that have insufficient members to be granted status as congregations. Stakes are presided over by a *stake presidency* consisting of the stake president and his two counselors. Financial affairs are coordinated by a *stake bishopric* consisting of the stake bishop and his two counselors. Congregations and missions are presided over by *presiding elders.*

Chart B

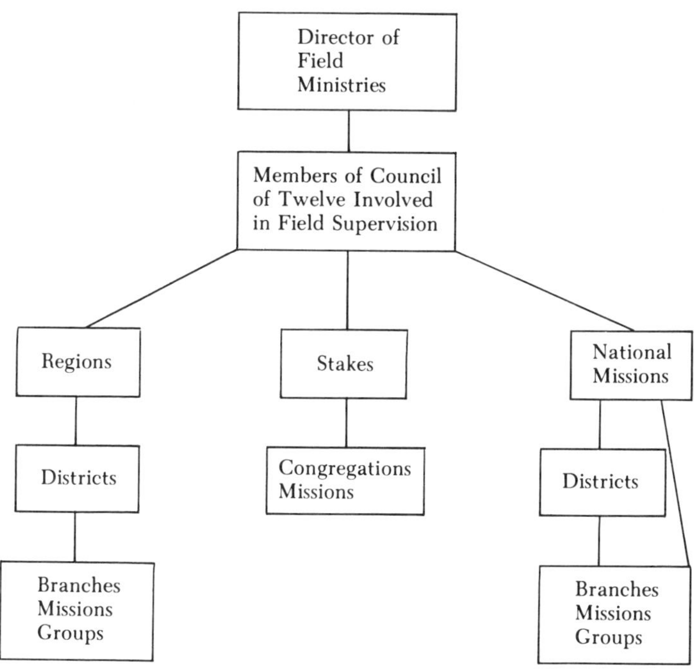

Regions are designated in such a way that most of the remainder of the United States and Canada lies within them. In 1976 there were thirteen regions, each including between one and ten states or provinces in the United States or Canada. Each region is presided over by a *regional administrator.* Within regions, *districts* are organized where reasonable geographic proximity makes this possible. While a region may be as much as a thousand miles from one side to another, in districts rarely more' than two hundred miles separates any two local units. A *district presidency* of three presides over the district. Whereas a stake is intended to be a single unit, a district is a collection of local church units called *branches.* Smaller units called *missions* and *groups* are also found in districts. A branch usually maintains its own building and it determines its own program. A *branch president* (often called a *pastor*) is elected to preside over the branch.

In addition to the standard stake and regional forms of organization, some areas are designated as "development areas" or "unorganized areas" because there are insufficient members and local units to justify the organization of a district or stake. Where there is a concentration of several hundred members in a metropolitan area, a *metropolitan branch* may be organized. This usually consists of several congregational units. The map on pages 120-121 shows the distribution of church membership in the United States and Canada.

The total membership of the Saints Church was 212,423 on June 30, 1975. Chart C on page 119 indicates the approximate membership in each country where members are located. Church or-

CHART C

Distribution of Saints Church Membership by Country, June 30, 1975.

Argentina	23
Australia	4,256
Brazil	67
British Isles	1,672
Canada	11,118
Denmark	17
Fiji	35
French Polynesia	3,307
Germany	975
Grand Cayman	54
Haiti	1,113
Honduras	85
India	886
Japan	95
Korea	255
Mexico	365
Netherlands	483
New Caledonia	132
New Zealand	243
Nigeria	1,699
Norway	37
Peru	83
Philippines	319
United States	157,778
Sweden	13
Other Countries	225
Unknown	27,088
Total Membership	212,423

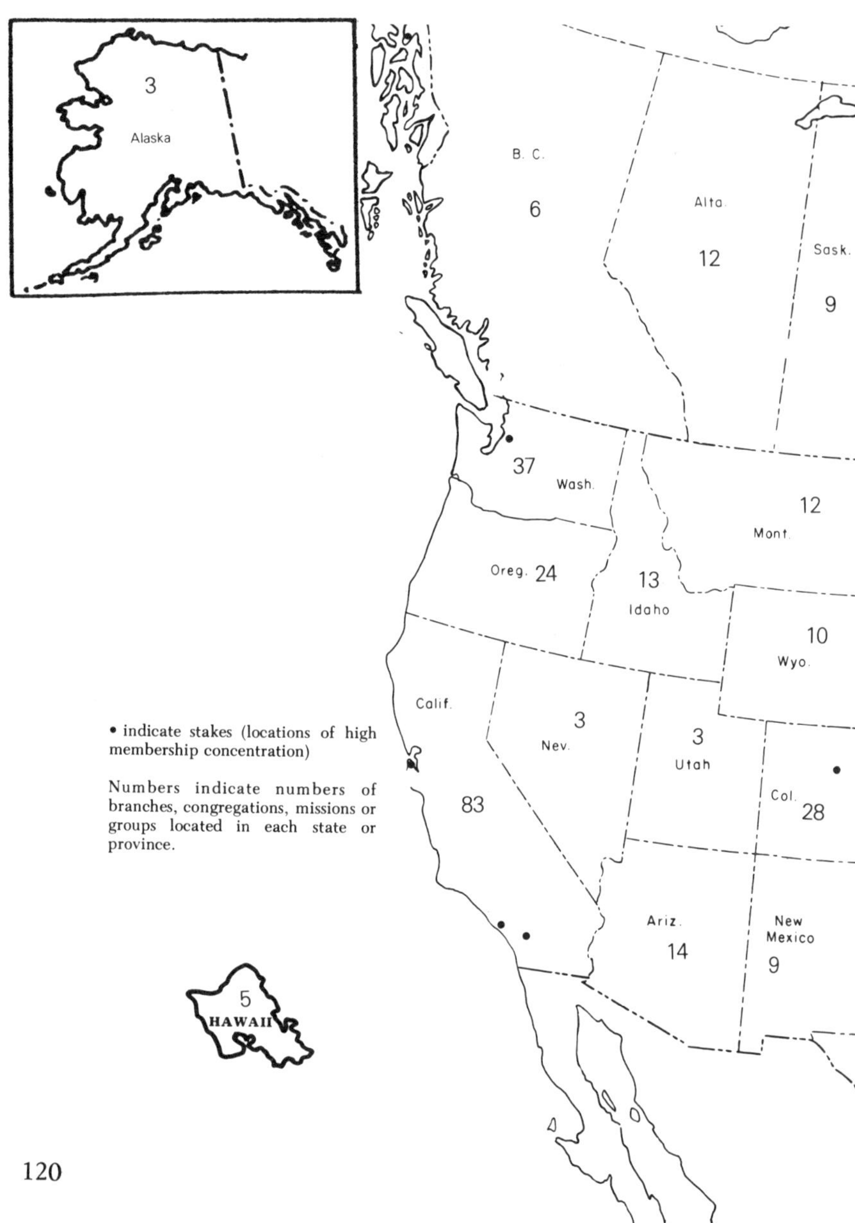

• indicate stakes (locations of high membership concentration)

Numbers indicate numbers of branches, congregations, missions or groups located in each state or province.

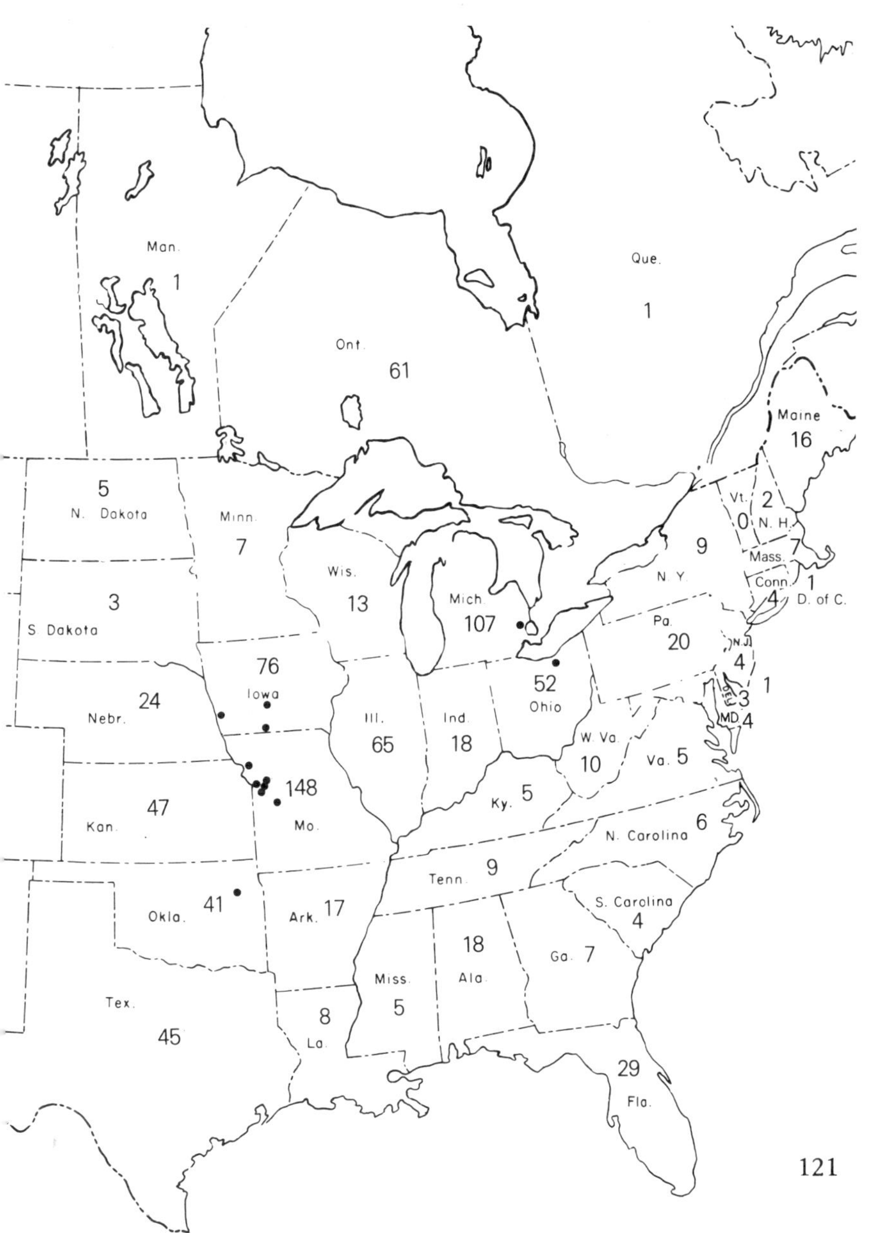
Man.
1
Que.
1
Ont.
61
Maine
16
5
N. Dakota
Minn.
7
Vt.
0
2
N. H.
9
Mass.
7
Wis.
13
Mich.
107
N. Y.
Conn.
4
1
D. of C.
3
S. Dakota
Pa.
20
76
Iowa
N.J.
4
24
Nebr.
52
Ohio
1
DEL
3
MD.
4
Ill.
65
Ind.
18
W. Va.
10
Va.
5
148
Mo.
47
Kan.
Ky.
5
N. Carolina
6
Tenn.
9
Okla.
41
Ark.
17
S. Carolina
4
18
Ala.
Ga.
7
Miss.
5
Tex.
45
8
La.
29
Fla.

ganization in countries other than Canada and the United States takes the form of *national missions.* Each is presided over by a *mission president.* The various branches, missions, and groups are usually related directly to the Mission except in Australia and England where districts are organized as in North America. The map on page 123 shows the location of membership worldwide.

FINANCIAL SERVICES. The *Presiding Bishopric,* consisting of the presiding bishop and his two counselors, supervises the financial operations of the church. They relate broadly to the functions of fund-raising, budget control, and maintenance of assets. The Presiding Bishopric maintains relationships with bishops, bishop's agents, and solicitors who care for financial affairs in the field jurisdictions of the church. Financial services are also available from the church headquarters. These include data management, financial management counseling and education, budget preparation, advice regarding church building construction and many other related services. The Presiding Bishopric also acts as trustee for all church properties and assists in the management of various church-related institutions within the city of Independence, Missouri.

Certain funds collected by field jurisdictions are forwarded to the Presiding Bishopric through its local representatives. The internal financial operations of these jurisdictions are, however, managed by their own elected treasurers. In stakes and regions, a bishop serves the dual role of local agent and custodian of World Church funds and properties as well as treasurer and custodian of local finances.

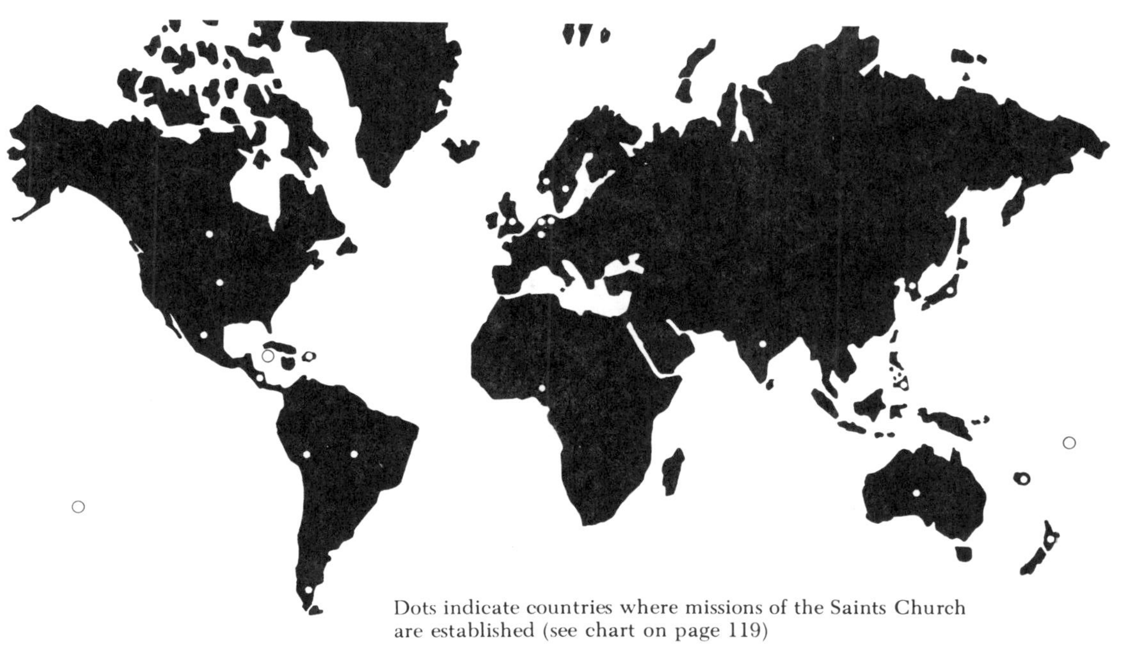

Dots indicate countries where missions of the Saints Church are established (see chart on page 119)

ADMINISTRATIVE SERVICES. This function is concerned with field organization planning and ministerial personnel and training. It is supervised by the director of the Division of Administrative Services. This division is responsible for developing, recommending, and implementing programs and policies in two basic areas. The first is *field organization* which has to do with the development and organization of the various field jurisdictions. The second area is *ministerial personnel* which relates to developing and administering policies for recruitment, education, assignment, job definition, and performance appraisal of persons working full time in ministerial responsibility.

PROGRAM SERVICES. This function is concerned with the use of communications through which the objectives, programs, and interpretations of the church's ministry can be shared. It is supervised by the director of the Division of Program Services. There are three commissions in the Program Services Division. The *Pastoral Services Commission* is responsible for the production of resources and providing of consultant services which can be used by the field jurisdictions in their programs. These resources are produced and made available by the Christian Education, Leadership, Pastoral Care, and Worship Offices, the Music Department, and the Family Ministry and Campus Ministry consultants. The *Communications Commission* provides Broadcasting and Audio-Visual services and is also responsible for historic properties, guide services, a museum, and Public Information Office. These services help to convey the message of the church to the public at large. This commission also works with the Pastoral Services Commission in developing appropriate resources for use in the church. The *Women's Ministry Commission* is concerned with the production of resources and provision of consultant services on the subject of ministry with, by, and for women. An important aspect of its task is the exploration of potentials and opportunities for women in the life of the church and in society at large.

PROGRAM PLANNING. This function is concerned with various areas which contribute to the overall planning task of the church. It is supervised by the director of the Division of Program Planning. This division is concerned with coordinating and integrating the various ministries of the church into a unified whole. Within the division are three commissions. The *Theology Commission* attempts to keep the church's theological interpretations abreast with the times and the social characteristics that are apparent. The *Zionic Community Commission* works at defining the characteristics of Zionic community life and of the Zionic ideal. The *Evangelism Commission* concerns itself with developing appropriate images of the church's ministry of outreach and how the church witnesses to the saving power of Jesus Christ as well as to its own traditions.

In addition to these three commissions, the Program Planning Division contains the *History Department.* Assisting the Church Historian in this department are persons responsible for archival and library services. The *Basic Beliefs Committee* works closely with the Theology Commission and is also a part of the Program Planning Division. The director of the Program Planning Division also convenes the *Execu-*

tive Planning Committee with representatives drawn from the other divisions and functions. This committee acts in an advisory way in the development of plans for the entire church.

PATRIARCHAL MINISTRIES. The *Presiding Patriarch* presides over the Order of Evangelists (Patriarchs). He keeps a central file of all patriarchal blessings given and keeps in touch with patriarchs in the field through a periodic newsletter. Patriarchs function throughout the church in giving blessings and performing evangelistic ministries. There are approximately 250 patriarchs throughout the church but with no consistent pattern of distribution.

Even though these six functions have certain defined responsibilities, overall coordination is important in the administration of the church. To assist in providing this coordination the *Interdivisional Council* meets monthly. This council brings together in dialogue personnel from each of the six functions. It provides opportunity for the various directors, commissioners, and other personnel to become acquainted with the tasks being performed by other offices. It also acts as a sounding board for new ideas.

Various combinations of the First Presidency, Council of Twelve, and Presiding Bishopric meet together several times each year to consider issues of major policy and church-wide management. One important function of the First Presidency, Council of Twelve, and Presiding Bishopric when meeting as a joint council is the approval and assignment of persons to World Church appointment. Appointees, as these persons are called, are those who give full time to the work of the church and in return receive financial support for themselves and their families. They help the church fulfill its worldwide mission. At the present time, there are about two hundred World Church appointee ministers. These include the First Presidency, Council of Twelve Apostles, Presiding Bishopric, Presiding Patriarch, Division Directors, Commissioners, and selected other headquarters staff. They also include missionaries reaching out to persons in areas where the church is being established, jurisdictional officers in stakes and regions, and others assigned to field and specialized responsibilities throughout the church.

Appointees are transferred to different responsibilities by action of the three presiding quorums; the average term of assignment varies according to a particular responsibility and the needs of the church. Appointees submit annual family allowance budget requests and are paid a monthly allowance based on cost of living in area of residence, size of family, and other variables. The appointee himself is provided with a car, used primarily in relation to his ministry, and an expense account for his official expenditures. Normal retirement for appointees comes at the age of sixty-five after which financial support for the appointee and his wife is provided by the church retirement program and other applicable sources. At the present time all appointees are members of the Melchisedec priesthood, the specific assignment being related to the particular office to which each is ordained.

The headquarters divisions and related institutions are largely staffed by full-time salaried executives. In addition, some stakes, regions, and national missions employ personnel to care for various functions.

LEGISLATIVE FUNCTIONS

The government of the Saints Church is by the principle of common consent. The term "theocratic democracy" has sometimes been used to emphasize that the church is both God's church and the people's church. The democratic process is employed in making decisions in the church. All administrative functions and positions described earlier in this chapter are subject to the legislative process. This means that *all* administrators hold office and perform their functions by being elected or sustained by the people voting in legislative assemblies.

At the highest legislative level is the *World Conference*. This assembly presently meets once every two years in the spring and lasts one week. Delegates are elected by field jurisdictions on a ratio of one delegate per one hundred members. Presiding officers of all field jurisdictions, members of the high priesthood, headquarters staff executives, and selected other persons act as ex officiis with full voice and voting rights. The World Conference sustains all appointees and headquarters administrative officers. It also approves the World Church budget which is used to support appointees and their families, finance church endeavors in national missions, support church institutions (e.g. Graceland College and the Independence Sanitarium and Hospital), build and maintain headquarters buildings, finance the operations of the various commissions and divisions of the First Presidency's staff, and meet other expenditures approved by the Conference. The Conference also receives reports from the various quorums, councils, divisions, commissions, and committees summarizing their accomplishments over the two-year period. The

World Conference makes policy statements or *Conference Resolutions* as they are called. These relate to the functioning of the church and to individual and corporate moral and ethical issues.

One important responsibility of the World Conference is to act on inspired documents presented to it by the president of the church in his role as "prophet, seer, and revelator" to the church. Documents are presented to the various quorums, orders, councils, and assemblies before being formally brought before the delegates for action. After being approved, documents are certified for inclusion in the Doctrine and Covenants. Members of the First Presidency, Council of Twelve, Presiding Bishopric, and the Presiding Patriarch are traditionally called to their responsibilities by being so named by the president in inspired documents. Such documents also indicate when persons are to be retired from these responsibilities. Other church officers are named and assigned by the First Presidency or Joint Council, all officers being subject to the sustaining vote of the Conference every two years.

National missions, regions, stakes, districts, branches, congregations, missions, and groups also hold legislative sessions. Similar functions to those described for the World Conference are also part of these lower jurisdictions' legislative agendas. Officers are elected and sustained; reports are received; budgets are approved. Other miscellaneous items of business are also transacted. Business sessions in these various jurisdictions are held annually or more frequently with the exception of regions that are only recently becoming seen as legislative units. All church members in good standing who are members of the jurisdictions concerned are eligible to vote in these legislative sessions. The only exception is for regional conferences to which elected delegates are sent. District, stake, and national mission conferences also elect delegates to the World Conference.

The legislative function provides opportunity for all members to participate in the decision-making process. They join in the formation of policy and program and assist in choosing leaders to whom they grant power to make short-term decisions of various kinds.

JUDICIAL PROCESS

Provision is made in church organization for the exercise of judicial process on the rare occasions that this becomes necessary. There are times when it appears to be in the best interests of the church that certain persons holding priesthood office be *silenced*. This means that their right to function in the office to which they are called and ordained is suspended or removed.

It is also the unpleasant duty of the church to excommunicate or expel members of the church from time to time. *Excommunication* means that the right to vote in legislative sessions and to partake of the emblems of the Lord's Supper is taken away. The excommunicated member is, however, still a member but is not "in good standing." *Expulsion* means that a person's membership is taken away. Such persons are no longer members of the church. Neither of these actions is taken without judicial process. Special courts are convened to consider the charges, evidence, and defense. The worth and dignity of the person concerned is always of major importance.

The primary objective of these actions is to promote repentance and reconciliation. The actions described here are taken only after intense effort has been made to bring about changes in attitude and behavior on the part of the persons involved. They are used only as a last resort when all else fails.

Church law also provides for the return of licenses to silenced priesthood members, reinstatement of excommunicated persons to full membership privileges, and for rebaptism of expelled members. These actions are possible when circumstances are such that it would be within the best interests of the person in question and of the church at large.

The administrative, legislative, and judicial processes of church organization are each important. They are interrelated in such a way as to provide balance and a corrective to possible abuses in power. Each process, seen in the context of the others, serves to facilitate the ongoing ministries of the church.

CHAPTER 12

HOW THE CHURCH LIVES

In the last two chapters we have looked at the meaning of calling as it applies to all members of the church as well as to those who are designated to fulfill specific functions. We have looked at the ways in which the church celebrates its meaningful events and recalls its history through the sacraments. We have also taken a brief look at the organizational structure of the church. It is the intent of this chapter to present a less formal glimpse of the life of the Saints Church. If persons were to associate themselves with the Saints, what kind of experience should they expect? What typical activities would they be involved in? What would be expected of them?

THE CHURCH GATHERED

In Chapter 9 it was noted that the church gathers together so that its members can share their common history and mission and be strengthened for their work on God's behalf in the world. In gathering the Saints involve themselves in four functions: worship, education, pastoral care, and stewardship. Let us look at each one of these in greater detail. In doing this we shall be describing some of the activities of local branches and congregations of the church. With over one thousand of these local units operating separately it is impossible to accurately describe what goes on in each. It is possible, however, to make some generalizations regarding activities and programs that are widespread throughout the church.

In the United States and Canada the Saints traditionally meet for public *worship* on Sunday mornings. Formerly services were also held on Sunday evenings with regularity. In recent years, however, many jurisdictions of the church are either holding Sunday evening worship services just once or twice each month, developing alternative activities, or forgoing Sunday evenings altogether. Practices in other countries are determined by local needs and customs. In many cases the Sunday morning services are designed for youth and adults with a separate "junior church" program being available for children. The Saints have traditionally avoided what is usually called a "liturgical" form of worship where set prayers and readings are spoken by minister and/or congregation. The most common form of Sunday morning worship is the preaching service which lasts approximately one hour and includes a sermon about thirty minutes long. Congregational hymn singing is used widely. Scriptures from the Bible, Book of Mormon, and Doctrine and Covenants are read and extemporaneous prayers are spoken. These are almost always done by members of the priesthood who preside from a platform at the front of the church sanctuary. The typical sanctuary is simply designed with the pulpit as the central focus. The Saints place little emphasis on visual symbolism; the officiating priesthood members usually wear business suits. Congregations use choirs and vocal or occasionally instrumental soloists, quartets, and other expressions of art where persons with the necessary talents can be found.

The sacrament of the Lord's Supper (Eucharist) has always been important in the life of the church. It is most often celebrated on the first Sunday of each month in place of the preaching service.

A midweek prayer and testimony service is traditionally held on Wednesday evenings. These services usually last an hour with at least half of the time available for prayers or testimonies from members of the congregation. Other types of worship services are held from time to time, mainly on special occasions such as Christmas and Easter.

In recent years more varied worship services are being planned for local churches. This is often at the insistence of youth, young adults, and others who feel that monologue sermons alone no longer fulfill their worship needs. The emphasis in these alternative styles of worship is on more opportunity for active participation of the members of the congregation. Other features include the use of modern religious songs and a wider use of arts such as drama.

Use of the Christian calendar with its various seasons is now becoming more widespread. To a significant extent, however, it is still ignored along with other worship forms and emphases that have characterized the Christian Church over the years. The Saints Church is just beginning to realize the potential for the use of unordained persons of various ages in worship.

For many years *education* has been formally expressed through the church school or Sunday school. In the United States and Canada this is usually held weekly on Sunday mornings. Most often church school is held for an hour starting at 9:30 or 9:45 a.m. with the worship service starting at 11:00 a.m. Formerly church school was nearly always divided into two periods. A fifteen- to twenty-minute worship period was followed by a forty-five- to sixty-minute class period. In recent years the worship period has declined in popularity in some places and has been replaced by an informal fellowship period, sometimes with refreshments. In other local churches the class period occupies the whole church school time block. Many churches, however, continue these two periods as described.

For many years the church headquarters has provided graded curriculum resources for use in classes for children and youth. Local churches are free to adapt the resources to their needs and even to choose materials from other sources when the official materials are found to be inappropriate to their needs. Church schools use volunteer teachers drawn mostly from the adult members of the congregation. The purpose of the curriculum resources and local class experiences is to provide children and youth with an overview of basic Christian and denominational understandings. The focus is on active discipleship at all ages of development. In recent years curriculum materials have emphasized the learning activity approach rather than the lecture approach for all ages.

Many church schools have few if any students other than those from the families of members of the Saints Church. Others, however, have been quite successful in attracting friends from their surrounding communities. In some cases the church school has become an important evangelistic tool.

Church schools also include classes for adults. Books and other resource materials are recommended for study by adults. These used to be written exclusively by members of the Saints Church and published by the church. More recently, however, other good resources have been recommended. Headquarters staff members prepare study guides which provide suggestions for the use of these materials in class settings. Local churches offer between one and six adult classes depending on the total number of adults attending. Classes usually have fewer than thirty members—often fewer than ten in small churches.

Formal education occurs in settings other than the church school. Weekend retreats, special classes and seminars, and small group discussions are other settings where education occurs. However, there is no regular pattern and these activities are usually scheduled as special events.

In our discussion of worship and education we have confined ourselves to planned activities. Education and worship also occur at times when they are not specifically planned. There is a sense in which the whole of life is an education. We learn at times when we least expect to learn. This is also true of worship. Although we see worship as basically a corporate event, the mood of worship is experienced by individuals and groups at times other than when they are assembled in a church sanctuary. Informality also characterizes the functions of pastoral care and stewardship. In fact these functions are carried on in the Saints Church more frequently in an informal sense than as a result of specific planning.

Pastoral Care is an important element in the life of the church. This function is closely related to the second of the six objectives of the church: the worth of persons. It is the recognition that each member is responsible for the life of others. The need for pastoral care stems from the realities of a technological age in which relationships have become more and more impersonal. Pastoral care is more a description of a way of life than it is a specific program.

A caring style of life is one in which members are sensitive to the needs of others and where an environment of open sharing with others is cultivated. Pastoral care might more appropriately be termed "congregational care," "personal care," or just "care." It is not the responsibility of the pastor or a few leaders. Pastoral care is the responsibility of all. It is first a preventive ministry. It attempts to prevent alienation and conflict between individuals. But because these separations inevitably occur, it is also a ministry of reconciliation. Pastoral care brings people together, settles differences, and restores unity.

Even though pastoral care is a style of life rather than a program it needs to be consciously built into programs and activities if such care is to become a reality. In many places the Saints are becoming more conscious of this need. One evidence of this is an increased concern for programming that provides for the interaction of persons of all ages in one setting. Persons are seen *first* as *persons* and second as children, youth, or adults. The recent emphasis on increased participation of members of all ages in worship and in decision-making in the local church is another evidence of concern for unity and the worthful contribution of each person.

Each local church exercises *stewardship* over the resources entrusted to it. Each jurisdiction holds a business meeting annually, or more often, at which decisions are made regarding the use of personnel (election of officers) and finances (adoption of budget). More local churches have recently involved themselves in the important processes of goal-setting, strategy development, and evaluation. This is another deliberate attempt to exercise responsible stewardship over the church's resources.

Emphasis is placed, usually in the setting of public worship, on individual and family finances. Most frequently this takes the form of special days on which annual tithing statements* or special offerings are received. In addition, sermons are preached exhorting the members to take seriously the call to respond to God's love by using wisely all that they have. Priesthood visiting usually focuses on stewardship early in each year. This concept of stewardship will be explored in more detail in Chapter 16.

The four gathered functions of the life of the church are also evident in various other programs and organizations found in the local groups of the Saints Church. Many local churches sponsor *Skylarks* (for girls six through nine), *Orioles* (for girls ten and eleven), *O-Teens* (for girls twelve through fourteen), *Scouts* (for boys and girls six through seventeen), *Zion's League* (senior high youth), *Zioneers* (junior high youth), and various other groups. Usually these organizations meet weekly at the church building or at the home of a member with one or more adult leaders present. Participants involve themselves in a variety of worship, study, fellowship, recreation, and service activities. Groups are sometimes organized for older youth, young adults, middle adults, and senior adults.

A popular organization in the local church has always been the women's department. This is no doubt

---

*See page 172.

due in part to the fact that a high percentage of the active men are members of the priesthood. These men meet together to concern themselves with worship, home visiting, and other church functions. In earlier years when few women worked outside the home, weekly women's department meetings were held during the daytime on a weekday. Recently, however, women's meetings are more often held in the evenings.

With the advent of the women's movement, the role of women in the Saints Church is being reevaluated. As part of its report to the 1974 World Conference, the First Presidency encouraged all jurisdictions of the church to provide for wider participation of women in the life of the church. Such wider participation is already becoming evident, particularly in decision-making, public worship, and on various committees. At the same time the role of the traditional women's department is undergoing reevaluation.

Summertime offers increased possibility for outdoor activities. The Saints have a rich tradition of camps of various kinds. One of these is the *reunion*. This is a family camp where persons of all ages gather for a week of worship, study, recreation, and fellowship. Reunions are usually held at church-owned or rented campgrounds. Some grounds are quite undeveloped and persons sleep in tents and trailers. Most, however, include cabins or dormitories, dining halls, meeting rooms of various kinds, and recreational facilities. These same campgrounds are also used for youth camps. Camps for senior high and junior high youth are widespread throughout the church. Some jurisdictions also conduct camps for children under the age of twelve. Camps for handicapped children and youth and for persons of minority groups are also held in some places.

THE CHURCH SCATTERED

So far we have dwelt almost completely on the gathered life of the Saints Church. It is now time to look at the scattered life. This is that phase of the church's life where it reaches outward in evangelistic and Zion-building endeavors.

Evangelism is at the heart of the church. The Saints, from the early years of their organization, have been anxious to share their testimonies of the gospel with others. Historically, the Book of Mormon has played an important role in these evangelistic endeavors. This was particularly true in the early years of the church during the lifetime of Joseph Smith. In recent years the church has conducted a reevaluation of the meaning of evangelism. Out of this has emerged a reaffirmation of the belief that the gospel is witnessed primarily in acts of loving concern for others. The Saints realize that any verbal sharing of beliefs and doctrine is fruitless unless accompanied by an active presence as the body of Christ.

A key ingredient of the evangelistic witness has always been the personal sharing of oneself with others on an individual basis. This occurs as Saints interact with others on the job, in the home, across the back fence, or in any of numerous other points of contact. While it is often tempting to persuade others to join the church, the sensitive member realizes that friendship is the important and prime prerequisite to any discussion of religious matters. Sound evangelistic procedures permit God to work in the lives of other people in ways consistent with their freedom and God's purpose.

Evangelism is more than a one-to-one endeavor. The perceptive Christian recognizes that the organizations and social structures of our societies need to be transformed into the kingdom of God. This is what we call *Zion-building.* In terms of community ministries, the Saints are found active in both individual and corporate ways. As individuals they endeavor in their vocations to make the business world a better place for everyone. In politics they support and work for the election of candidates who make the needs of the people their highest priority. Some run for, are elected, and serve in political office. When they do this, their fellow Saints and their constituents are justly proud and expect achievements of note to result from their efforts. Some members work with other persons to accumulate funds to erect hospitals, nursing homes, and other public service facilities. Other Saints are active in civic organizations and neighborhood programs that are directed toward the betterment of the communities in which they live. Some serve as volunteers in inner-city ministries or on health teams to developing countries. Others are simply known as friendly neighbors who are quick to lend a helping hand when the need arises.

In the early days of the church when the Saints were on the geographic frontier in America they worked corporately to establish communities principled after their ideas of the kingdom of God. In modern times, with the rapidly expanding population in most parts of the world, their joint efforts have become much more diffused. When an institution constitutes a very small minority of the citizens of a community its influence may hardly be felt. For this reason the Saints' Zion-building efforts in recent years have been primarily individual or jointly with members of other organizations. An important exception is in the stakes where concentrations of members work together to improve the conditions of their communities. More and more local groups of Saints are providing personnel and financial resources for community betterment. Objections to Christians becoming involved in politics and community affairs are giving way to a greater openness to working among the people and structures of the world. Examples of corporate Zion-building efforts are the establishment of adoption agencies, day care centers, and new rest homes for the elderly.

We have had opportunity for only a brief look at the evangelism and Zion-building functions of the church. These will be treated in greater detail in chapters 14 and 15.

CHAPTER 13

WHERE IS THE WORLD GOING?

Each of us thinks about the future. For some, the future is only occasionally of concern. It is fairly often on the minds of others. For still others, the subject is of constant concern. A very simple decision to take some meat out of the freezer in the morning so that it will be defrosted for cooking by evening reflects thought about the future. We could call this short-term planning. A decision to begin purchasing life insurance at an early age also reflects thought about the future. We could call this long-term planning. In between the short-term and long-term are numerous decisions that help determine our lives during the months and years ahead. Many short-term decisions are made automatically and if mistakes occur the consequences are often minor. Long-term decisions, on the other hand, are usually made after careful consideration of the issues involved and often have major consequences. The point is that we cannot live in the present without at the same time acting to determine our future. In addition, we all have conscious or subconscious feelings about the future—feelings of hope or of despair or both. It is the purpose of this chapter to consider various alternative views of the future. Then we will look at the attitude demonstrated by Jesus and the church down through the years.

HOW DO WE FEEL ABOUT THE FUTURE?

At the risk of oversimplifying, we can identify two basic ways of viewing the future. First, the world can be seen as corrupt and completely without hope. This is the "stop the world, I want to get off" view. Those holding this view wish to keep themselves as far away from the world's evils as possible. They may attempt to isolate themselves as much as they can from other people and things; the best thing to do is patiently wait for the end of history. This view sees contemporary evidences of natural disasters, wars, famines, and other catastrophes to be signs of the coming end. Second, the world can be seen to possess hope and possibility. This view suggests that in spite of tragedies and failures the world has potential. Persons holding this view participate fully in the affairs of the world, feeling confident that they can make contributions toward its betterment. They see the present as a challenge in which they can profitably invest their resources. These people carry with them a spirit of realistic optimism. They face the future with a realistic view of its possibilities.

Do you see yourself in one or both of these views? To some extent, we all do. The two views are, perhaps, extremes. Many of us feel a mixture of optimism and pessimism about the future, of hope and despair. This is understandable. For any one of us, our view of the future may change as the circumstances of our lives change. It is not unusual, for example, to experience deep despair and pessimism immediately following a major catastrophe such as war or starvation or the loss of a loved one. With the passage of time our view becomes more hopeful as we emerge from preoccupation with the event.

WHAT DOES THE GOSPEL SAY ABOUT THE FUTURE?

In Chapter 3 we reflected briefly on the various attitudes that frequently characterize our humanity. In Chapter 4 we pointed toward salvation through Jesus Christ. We reaffirm here that God through his Son has won victory over wrong for all time. This has often been misinterpreted. It is not suggesting that God has eliminated all evil from the world. We know this isn't so because we frequently experience evil in our daily lives. By permitting us freedom of choice, God permits evil to be present. He does not promise to take it away. Instead he promises us the power and strength to cope with it. A just God could not take away the natural consequences of our unwise decisions. Living with the consequences helps us to learn. Through experience we realize that acting in kindness and concern toward others makes our lives more satisfying than selfishly pursuing our own interests. To say that God through Jesus Christ has won the battle over evil means that life characterized by love is infinitely more worthwhile than life dominated by evil.

What we have said does not deny that wrong is continually challenging right in new battles every day. We know that this is so. God's victory is a victory for all time in that whenever right meets wrong God comes through victorious. This principle is most forcibly illustrated by Jesus' resurrection. In this most significant event God proved that Jesus' crucifixion was not the final word on the subject. He said that the quality of life that Jesus lived was not subject to the evil motives of those who shouted "Crucify him!" It would certainly have appeared that wrong had been victorious if Jesus' crucifixion had been the final event in his life. Instead God reaffirmed the validity of good as expressed in Jesus' life. Through the resurrection, life wins over death, right over wrong.

Our daily encounters with right and wrong are very real. Many times evil appears to emerge as the winner. But God is continually with us. His love has the power to forgive and to give new life. This is really what resurrection is all about. We all experience the realities of evil in our lives, situations that "take the life out of us." A sound belief in a living God makes it possible to reach out and grasp new life which completely changes our attitude toward the future. Experiencing God's victory over evil gives us a hopeful view of things to come.

The accounts of Jesus' ministry in the Scriptures show him as frequently anticipating the coming of God's kingdom. He saw the future with hope. He anticipated a better way of life. He saw the freeing of the oppressed, the making whole of those who suffered. This note of hope has persisted in the Christian tradition down through the centuries. Immediately following Jesus' earthly ministry his followers anticipated his early return—a time when Jesus would rule over the world. Down through the years, Christians and non-Christians have given attention to the task of creating a better world. Theoretical approaches have yielded numerous volumes on the subject. Practical attempts to build model communities have succeeded and failed in varying degrees. The ideal has persisted—an ideal founded on a basic optimism that a better future is possible.

The Saints Church was founded in the United States at a time of high interest in Utopian communities. Specific efforts in this direction will be discussed in the next chapter. It is important to say here, however, that Latter Day Saintism has always viewed the kingdom of God as existing in this world. The Saints have tried to resist the temptation to view God's kingdom as a separate existence in the future after this world has come to an end. Emphasis on a "this-worldly" kingdom led the Saints to concern themselves early with the realities of the "secular" world. They organized their affairs in ways consistent with what they understood to be God's purposes for them. They use the term "Zion" to refer to a tangible expression of God's kingdom on earth. Various interpretations and aspects of Zion will be treated in the next chapter.

This emphasis on God's kingdom in this world has resulted in two other important understandings. First, the Saints have traditionally denied the validity of a separation of the sacred and the secular. The view supporting such a separation says that the world and all that is in it is "material" and evil. On the other hand, God is righteous and the religious lives of people, in which they relate to God, are "spiritual." Taken to the extreme this view affirms that each person has a sinful body and a righteous spirit. By affirming that God's kingdom is an expression of righteousness among the everyday world, the Saints deny this artificial distinction. God calls us to approach *all* phases of our lives with the loving concern that Jesus shared. The truest expressions of Christian discipleship are found in the home, in school, on the job, among friends as well as in the church building on Sundays.

Second, the present-life focus of God's kingdom has caused the Saints to approach speculation regarding the afterlife with caution. It is very comforting for us to be certain about the future. Indeed we *can* be certain about the future but not in the way some people think. One of the basic principles of the Christian belief in God is faith. The Hebrews learned some painful lessons about faith. They thought that God should not lead them anywhere without first telling them exactly where they were going. For them, faith meant knowing in advance what would happen to them. This was not to be the case. God told them to march into the wilderness in a direction totally opposite to the promised land to which they thought he was leading them. They learned that faith is not so much knowing the unknown as it is believing in God and that he can be trusted.

This is the way it is with the afterlife. We would like to know exactly what will happen to us. But instead, God asks us to live with the certainty that he will provide for us. It would seem that there is no harm in speculating on what the future will be like. We all do it. It is when we view such speculations as "the truth" that problems arise. We affirm that God through his love provides for his human creation. He loves and cares for us in this life and has created us as persons of worth. For this reason we can have faith that he will provide for us in the future, whatever specific form that might take.

HOW CAN WE LIVE IN HOPE?

In response to the question "Why are you hopeful about the future?" one person replied, "Because it is easier to live life today being hopeful than it is to live in despair." On the surface this may seem to be an inadequate answer. However, we should not dismiss it lightly. Our feelings about the future contribute both to what our present lives are like and also to what life will be like for us in the future. We all know people who are unhappy today not because they are experiencing difficulty in the present but because they live in despair about the future. Such persons may be unfulfilled, experience self-hatred, and have difficulty relating to others. They have already decided that tomorrow is going to be "bad news" and so there is no point in doing anything constructive today. There is little to do other than feel depressed about what is to come. On the other hand, we also know people who are happy today not because everything is going right for them but because they are hopeful about the future. These people experience fulfillment and a sense of self-worth. They relate easily to others. They have decided that tomorrow is going to be "good news" and so they live confidently today in that expectation.

There are certainly other reasons for the way we behave in the present than our expectations about the future. For many of us present-day life experiences *are* predominant in determining how we act today. However, for others, our view of the future does make a difference in what we say and do now.

But one might easily say, "What's the use of feeling good about the future when we can't affect what will happen?" There are many who feel powerless to do anything about the future. They believe that everything has been predetermined. Some even go as far as saying that God has predestined each of us to heaven or hell and the most we can do is to find out which end will be ours. This view, however, appears to be a perversion of the idea of an all-powerful and all-knowing God. When we say that God has won victory over wrong for all time we are still left with the choice of what we will do with our lives. What we do today has *everything* to do with where we will be tomorrow. We are of course limited as to what we can do. We cannot grow six inches in height overnight. But we are not powerless, although many of us feel that way. Who we are today *is* affected by our decisions yesterday, and our decisions today affect who we will be tomorrow.

The gospel of Jesus Christ offers hope. It gives us the power to look expectantly toward the future. Every time our lives are touched by God's love experienced through others, we smile or shed a tear and know that a better future is possible. Likewise the gospel permits us to be open about the future. This requires risk and faith. Risk is present because we aren't sure what will happen to us. Faith is there when we trust in God who calls us to the unknown future. Hope and openness describe the stance of disciples who know that God stands with them in their uncertainty.

This all adds up to a reaffirmation of Jesus' emphasis on the coming kingdom of God. This is life ruled by God, where the forces of evil have no power. The ultimate destiny of history is the kingdom of God. There can be no other end. This is the hope in which we live—not just a dream that *might* come true but a hope that *will* materialize because God is Lord of the universe and of history.

CHAPTER 14

EVANGELISM

The literal meaning of the word "gospel" is good news. Evangelism is being alive in the good news that Jesus Christ is the Lord of all creation. As persons who have accepted the love of God demonstrated in Jesus Christ, we are called to go "into all the world" to share this good news of God's victorious love. The church as the body of Christ is called in all aspects of its corporate life to share the gospel. As individual disciples, as families, and as congregations we have the primary responsibility of sharing the gospel. Evangelism gives purpose and meaning to everything we are. Without evangelism the church ceases to exist.

WITNESSING OF JESUS CHRIST

The Saints Church rests on the cornerstone of God's initiative in life. When young Joseph Smith was confused over the conflicting claims of various religious teachers his understanding was opened to this imperative, "This is my Son—hear him." A few years later as leader of the newly formed church and in response to this invitation to "hear him" Joseph Smith affirmed, "After the many testimonies which have been given of him this is the testimony...which we give of him, that he lives...." (Doctrine and

Covenants 76:3g). The church is to proclaim the living Christ to all who will hear.

Evangelism provides a corrective for our personal and corporate idolatries. When we tend to "go our own way" and worship our self-made gods we need reminders. We need those who care enough about us to go out of their way to love us into repentance. It is God who initiates this loving process in our lives. In the Genesis story, when Adam and Eve disobeyed God and tried to hide, God came searching for them as if to say "Adam and Eve [representing all humankind], you cannot run away. You cannot make me stop loving and caring. I'm coming after you!"

The gospel, then, is God's initiative in our life! God created us and cares for us; desires the best for us; wants us to find fulfillment in life. In spite of our failings and shortcomings he still cares for us. By his nature he always forgives us and calls us to try again to be his faithful disciples. The gospel is the living evidence in Christ that God has entered into our presence, knows our human condition, takes our sin upon him, and leads us into new life. Through the life of faith and trust in Christ we are saved from inadequate images of self, and freed to become the sons and daughters of our Creator. Evangelism is the witnessing of this *good news* to all persons. Even those of us who have heard the message frequently forget it. When we are reminded we still find it hard to believe. We need to hear it time and time again.

THE EVANGELISTIC LIFE

The church plays a very important role in the transformation of persons. As the body of Christ, the church reaches out to those in need of love and assurance. It provides the environment in which persons are healed and made whole. We become disciples only in association with other disciples. We cannot be saved alone. There is no such experience as private salvation. Our experience or renewal in Christ calls us to share our new life with others. The church becomes a community of evangelists: those eager to share the love of God with all.

The church which acts like a hermit cannot be evangelistic. We become evangelistic by thrusting ourselves into the midst of life, where people are hurting; where they are needing healing; where there is alienation, fear, separation, and mistrust. We share there the quality of love which will heal the wounds of nations, of families, of husband and wife, and of parent and child. We have to pass on in human relationships far more than words about God, as important as those words are. We must share with other persons the very testimonies of our own lives. We must share the joy, happiness, sense of fulfillment, and purpose in life which we have discovered by coming in contact with Jesus Christ and with people who love him.

The admonitions which Jesus gave to his disciples when he sent them out into Israel on their first mission is sound advice for us today. He sent them out to heal the sick, to preach the gospel of deliverance, and then he said, "Freely ye have received, freely give." Sharing the good news is far more than just retelling the story of a Baby born in a stable in Bethlehem or how a church was organized. Relaying the good news of God's love for us means living in new relationships to others. It means establishing a new way of responding to those about us. It means meeting, communicating, touching others in a new way, for the good news is not good news until it becomes real in the way we live.

A most revealing statement about the quality of Jesus' love and compassion is found in the Scriptures. He was walking in a crowd and a woman reached out and touched the hem of his garment. Jesus asked, "Who touched me? Virtue has gone out of me." He was so sensitive to the needs of people that in the very act of touching his garment there was a transaction, a communication between him and that woman. He didn't even know who it was but he was so sensitive that something very naturally went out of him into her life just by that touch. That's the kind of sensitivity that we must have to the needs of one another if we are to be evangelists. We must open our hearts and our minds and our arms to one another and gladly share that which we have received. The best possible good news for many people is the realization that they are persons of worth, with no strings attached, because God loves them unequivocally and without reservation. There are many people alive today who do not believe they have worth because they have not experienced it in their lives.

The biblical concept of leaven can help us understand how we are to be evangelists. Leaven (yeast) reacts chemically with the ingredients of the whole loaf. Every molecule is chemically changed by the action of the leaven. Not only is the flavor improved but the appearance of the loaf is enhanced. When we are confronted with the reality of God's love our whole lives are affected. The apostle Paul said we become new persons in Christ. Our lives are not changed in just one aspect or in just certain relationships. We become not only different or better but *new* persons. The evangelist and the evangelistic church seek ways to transform persons and society through the leavening process.

NEWNESS OF LIFE

Newness of life is capsulized in two primary understandings which guide the life of the disciple: (A) The love of God is the center of life. (B) The worth of persons through God's grace becomes the focus of all relationships. Basic affirmations which arise from these two understandings are as follows:

1) God loves us and cares for us. He is the universal Creator. He has purpose in our lives. He is alive and available through Jesus Christ and the Holy Spirit.
2) Jesus Christ is the living expression of God, the Word made flesh. He is God's personal investment in human life. Scriptures enrich our understanding of Christ and his life in us. Revelation is shared through him in prophetic leadership and membership.
3) We are persons of great worth in the sight of God. We have been blessed with gifts, talents, abilities, and potential. We are called to participate in God's great cause.
4) Life is a great challenge and opportunity when lived in God's way. Life is a stewardship of responsive ministry. Life offers wholeness, joy, hope, and fulfillment when built on a trusting relationship with God.
5) Worship, especially through ordinance and sacrament, helps us to grow as disciples. The community of the faithful (the church) responds to Christ and persons. Spiritual growth results from this meaningful involvement.
6) The church is the community of the faithful—those who have responded to the gospel. As individuals we find enrichment and support in

this fellowship of Saints. The "body of Christ" seeks to fulfill the shared calling of representing him in the world.

7) Zionic community building invites our contributions (this will be expanded in Chapter 15). Community development expresses corporately God's will for each of us. Developing close trust relationships with others brings new meaning, purpose, hope, and joy to our lives.
8) God's mission can be expressed in and through us. Learning, doing, and being are blended together in service. Joining our lives with Christ's is a dynamic, continuous experience of growth and enrichment.

These affirmations provide a foundation upon which we as disciples and the church as the body of Christ reach out into the lives of persons and communities.

Evangelism is as much a style of life as it is a specific program. Within the Saints Church, however, certain deliberate approaches to sharing the gospel have been used over the years. Members have always been eager to share their testimonies with their friends. Nonmembers are invited to attend worship services, church school classes, and fellowship events. This informal approach gives persons an opportunity to share in the fellowship of the Saints and to be exposed to the community which means so much to the members.

Missionary preaching series have been used widely over the years. In such series, seventies or other ministers preach several sermons on church belief and practice within the space of a week. These sermons are held in the setting of worship services to which members invite interested friends. Another traditional setting for sharing the gospel with nonmembers is the cottage meeting. These meetings are held weekly in the homes of members and nonmembers and are designed to provide information and instruction in church beliefs and practice. In recent years other approaches have been more widely used.

Necessary though these formal introductions to the church are, they can never take the place of the hand of friendship extended by members to their friends. The essence of evangelism is still the life given in Christlike service to others. The life of the evangelist speaks of the victory of Christ, the power of his salvation, and the hope of the future as we go with him in faith. The gospel is not shared primarily in words. It is communicated in loving action and specific expressions of concern. The calling of the church to establish his kingdom includes a major commitment to demonstrate to the world what can be and what shall be when Jesus Christ takes first place in our lives. The leaven of the gospel is intended to transform persons and societies into a quality of living which is worthy to be called the kingdom of God. All are invited to participate in this important task.

CHAPTER 15

ZION

The ultimate destiny of history is the kingdom of God. We have referred to how the Saints have always seen God's kingdom as being "in this world." They have seen their ideas in terms of tangible expressions in the present life rather than in some "afterlife." This kingdom enterprise has been a consistent theme throughout Latter Day Saint history. The term used by the Saints to describe the kingdom and kingdom-building process is *Zion.* This term is found in the Old Testament where it is used to describe Jerusalem, the religious capital of the Jewish nation. This chapter will consider the role of the concept of Zion in the Saints Church. We will look at Zion from three different views. This is not to suggest that there are three alternative ways of looking at Zion. Rather we can say that all three are present to varying degrees in the belief of most members. We shall look at Zion as *place,* as *condition,* and as *process.*

ZION AS PLACE

For those who expect God's kingdom to be a reality only in the afterlife, concern about the actual location is minimal. It is sufficient to say that it is "in heaven" or "after death." For the Saints, who believe that

God's kingdom is in this world, however, concern over location is important. Where in this whole world or universe is God's kingdom to be located? Is there to be *one* location, *several*, or *many*? The church dealt with this question early in its life.

Wherever the Saints were gathered in sufficient numbers to make an impact on the community, kingdom-building was a dream, a possibility, and a reality. As early as 1831 the Saints began to build communities where their understanding of God's will could be expressed. The first was at Kirtland, Ohio. Begun in 1831, it included not only church-related enterprises but also small businesses to serve the needs of the Saints. Land acquisition was important and its use was planned with care. Later communities during the lifetime of Joseph Smith were begun in Independence and Far West in Missouri and at Nauvoo in Illinois. At Nauvoo, the Saints' concerns expanded into educational, political, and military affairs. No part of so-called "secular" existence was beyond the scope of concern of these pioneers. They saw the kingdom of God as encompassing *all* aspects of life, relating to the *whole* person. Building Zion meant taking the material resources available and developing structures that made it possible to live according to God's will.

These same principles of Zionic establishment are at the center of the Saints' outreach ministries today. In the 1830s and 1840s as the Saints moved westward from the east to the center of what is now the United States they were pioneers on the edge of a geographic frontier. This is well illustrated by the use of the term "Far West" as applied to one of the Saints' gathering places in Missouri. They moved into areas that were relatively undeveloped and sparsely populated. Their role was to build communities almost from scratch. Today there is very little undeveloped or sparsely populated territory (except barely usable deserts or mountains) in the United States or in other nations. Consequently, Zion-building today tends to emphasize the revitalization of existing communities where the Saints have residence. Nevertheless, small pilot communities are sometimes formed by associations of members acting on their own initiative.

In 1831, Joseph Smith designated Independence, Missouri, as the *Center Place.* This town was to be the center of Zionic development among the Saints. From it was to radiate the influence of God's kingdom to the entire world. Designation of Independence as the Center Place does not mean that this city is the only real location of Zion. Implied in the designation of a center is the existence of areas around. This has been recognized organizationally by the designation of other geographic areas as *stakes* of Zion. Neither does the designation of a center place imply that the center plays a more important role than other areas. The center has a unique role which no other area can play. But so do other places, including stakes, have their distinctive roles.

When Joseph Smith designated Independence as the Center Place, he did more than make a statement. The Saints purchased sixty-three acres of land and immediately designated a plot for the building of a temple. The temple was to serve as the center of activity for the community and for worldwide Zionic development. To this day, the Saints still regard Independence as the Center Place. Part of the original sixty-three acres of land is the site for present and future headquarters buildings. Within the city limits of Independence thousands of Saints are working to improve the community where they live. By doing this they are building Zion in a very real way, right where they live. The Saints are active in politics, education, business, civic and religious affairs. By building strength at the center, the Saints are able to give support to other areas where their brothers and sisters are engaged in similar endeavors. Outlying areas look to the Center Place for leadership, support, and encouragement.

Whether they are at or near the Center Place or in a far-off corner of the world, the Saints continue to give tangible expression to God's kingdom in the particular places where they live. The Zionic ideal of the Saints is not an unreachable "pie in the sky" or expectation of afterlife. Zionic communities are being developed now in places all over the world.

ZION AS A CONDITION

Any vision of the kingdom of God presupposes certain things about the quality of life within that kingdom. It is obvious that all communities of people do not qualify to be called Zion. In fact many of the characteristics of living which Jesus encountered among the people of his day he judged as inconsistent with the principles of the coming kingdom. The inflexibilities of a legalistic system resulted in many people being oppressed. Jesus spoke of freedom in the context of responsibility. Zion, then, is more than a place; it is also a condition—a way of life. What are the characteristics of Zionic living? What is the *condition* which permeates God's kingdom?

If God revealed one thing about himself in Jesus Christ it was that he loves us. Our children sing "Jesus loves me, this I know" and "Jesus loves the little children" from their very earliest years. It is not enough, however, that we merely accept God's love. It is imperative that we love others, too. This is necessary because it is through us that God's love is experienced by other people. This mood of love pervades the truly Zionic community. It is its distinctive characteristic. The condition of the kingdom is such that all organizations and relationships have as their major goal meeting the needs of the members of the community. Laws unnecessarily restricting the freedom of the individual will be absent. Arrangements will provide for harmonious life together in community. The prevalent attitude will be that of tolerance of all individuals and their beliefs. There will be a mood of outreach rather than of exclusiveness. The spirit of humility will be evident as people acknowledge God as the giver of all that they have. Individuals will be encouraged to develop their own uniqueness in cultivating their various talents. Each one will share in the responsibility to contribute to making life worthwhile. There will be an absence of the stress and strain resulting from a fiercely competitive life-style. Persons will see each other as brothers and sisters rather than as competitors.

Other characteristics of Zionic living could be enumerated. We used the future tense but do not mean to suggest that life today is completely devoid of these characteristics. To the extent that these describe the conditions in which we live we can say that Zion is a reality today. Neither will all Zionic communities exhibit the same characteristics. Each culture and subculture has its unique gifts and contributions to add to the worldwide development of Zion. Each will be a unique expression of the people who comprise it. Sharing between cultures provides opportunity for the enrichment of each. The condition of Zionic living is summed up in a statement found in the Inspired Version of the Bible: "And the Lord called his people, Zion, because they were of one heart and of one mind, and dwelt in righteousness; and there were no poor among them" (Genesis 7:23).

ZION AS A PROCESS

While we have been talking about Zion as place and condition we have been implying more than this. Our final view is that Zion is a *process* in which God and humankind participate together. If Zion is to be a reality and if it is a different existence than that under which we live, then we have to ask how it comes about. It is not appropriate to think of Zion materializing solely as a result of human effort. If it did we would call it the human kingdom rather than God's kingdom. Neither is it appropriate to see Zion as instituted by God without human effort. Both God and humankind participate in making the kingdom a reality. In recent years in the Saints Church the expressions "Zionizing" and "Zion-building" are rising in popularity. These depict Zion as a process by which conditions such as those mentioned in the previous section become more and more of a reality in our communities.

We have been tempted from time to time to view Zion as something that arrives suddenly, in the way many Christians expect the second coming of Christ. This view suggests that if we work hard enough toward developing the appropriate conditions, the time will come when the kingdom will appear. From this perspective Zion is not here today but will be here tomorrow. It also suggests that Zion will become a reality in one or more selected locations and not in other places.

The Saints are continually reminded, however, to broaden their understanding of Zion. One of the six objectives established by the church in 1973 is "to interpret the Zionic concept for our day in world terms and pursue the implementation of Zionic development." Zion is not an all-at-once matter. It is a process. A handbook prepared for local leaders of the Saints Church indicates that

> Zion-building grows from the realization that persons live not in isolation but in community and that their group relations and institutions stand in need of redemption. Zion-building is the mission of the church in and to the institutional structures of society, which seeks to alter those structures so that they become redemptive rather than demonic, humanizing rather than dehumanizing. It means the involvement of the church with the political, the economic, and the social conditions of society.—*Congregational Leaders Handbook*, Section 4, page 3.

This statement clearly considers Zion-building as a process. It refers to the Zionic endeavor as working toward reforming the structures of our communities. Our institutions determine the environment in which we live. Institutions can provide a helpful, caring environment or they can provide a damaging, alienating environment. Institutions are not formed or maintained without human effort. We have the power to determine what influence they will have on their surrounding communities. An integral part of the call to build Zion is the responsibility to work for change within institutions which will make them more life sustaining. The Saints have long realized the need to become involved in the everyday affairs of the communities where they reside. They serve in elective offices, accept appointment to civic responsibility, volunteer their time to social welfare agencies, and involve themselves in other worthy causes. Beyond this, they see their everyday vocations as avenues for the expression of Christian motives and principles. They are working toward more equitable treatment of employees in businesses where they work.

Zion is an endeavor that is continuous. Progress is gradual yet noticeable. The Saints are influential in the communities where they live. They are known as honest and concerned persons. They contribute to the betterment of society grounded in the confidence that the kingdom of God is the ultimate destiny of history. When Zion is seen as a process, there is a sense in which it is already here. Zion is a reality now as well as in the future. But the task is never complete. Zionic endeavor is always an imperative in every community where the Saints live. It is the way in which the church participates with God in his work in the world.

Zion-building is a corporate endeavor. More is accomplished by working with others than by working alone. Sometimes this takes the form of individual Saints working with other individuals or groups in the communities where they live. At other times a group or congregation of Saints works together on a particular project. Both of these methods bring effective results.

The assurance that God is ultimately victorious and that his kingdom will come permits us to view Zion in terms of judgment as well as promise. We are promised that the condition for which we strive will become a reality. This future reality serves also to judge the present as inadequate. The kingdom of God implies that the present situation is not one with which we are to be satisfied. It points to a better future.

The dream and reality of Zion are integral parts of the faith of the Saints. Individually and collectively they work to make the dream more of a reality in the places where they live. The dream is not a selfish desire for an abundant life for themselves, but rather a response to God's concern for all humanity. The Saints view Zion as one of the many blessings that God makes available to all people and invite all to join in making his kingdom a reality.

CHAPTER 16

STEWARDSHIP

Concern with the affairs of this world has led the Saints to accept with seriousness responsibility for the various resources in their possession. In the spirit of acknowledging him as creator, God is seen as owner and persons as stewards. This concept of stewardship has received continual emphasis from the earliest years of the church in the 1830s up to the present time. This chapter will explore various aspects of the principle of stewardship.

WHO ARE STEWARDS?

All people are stewards whether they acknowledge it or not. We cannot elect or choose to be stewards or not to be stewards. Stewardship is a description of the *relationship* between God and persons. When we recognize this relationship we adopt an *attitude* which characterizes our whole lives. The writer of Genesis indicates that it is God's desire that we "be fruitful, and multiply, and replenish the earth, and subdue it; and have dominion. . . over every living thing" (1:30, I.V.). By the very recognition of God as creator we at the same time acknowledge that we are stewards. God does not choose a few to administer the resources of his world. He chooses everyone. We all have things over which we are stewards. No two of us have the same resources but all of us are responsible and accountable.

Not only are we stewards as individuals but also as groups. Organizations have resources made available to them by their members. They do not use these resources for their own ends but rather to accomplish the purposes established by their members. Groups of all kinds, churches included, are stewards over resources entrusted to them.

What is being said, very simply, is that all individuals and groups have available to them resources which they use. Every day we make decisions about how these are used. The principle of stewardship says that we acknowledge that we are custodians rather than owners. We are accountable to God, the owner, for the way we use his resources. But more than this, we are partners with God in his great work of redeeming the whole world. He trusts us with an important role in this task.

OVER WHAT ARE WE STEWARDS?

We have used the word *resources.* This is a convenient term to describe all that we are and have. Let us consider some examples. First, and most important, God has given us life itself—the opportunity to live, with all the possibilities that come with it. Life is all-encompassing. In a sense we can say that life is all that we are given. All other things are parts of life. Life is the one thing that all human beings have in common. Those things that make up our lives, however, are different. We have both tangible and intangible possessions. The amounts and kinds that we have differ from one individual to the next.

With regard to material possessions, some of us are richer than others. This unequal distribution is caused by many factors. It is caused partly by differences in initiative, interest, talent, and education. It is also caused by differences in inherited wealth. Another factor is the level of wealth and technology of the country or region where we live. These individual differences are very real and permit some of us to live in luxury while others are at the brink of starvation. The principle of stewardship applies, however, to all of us regardless of how large or small our material possessions are.

We also possess "things that money can't buy." Just as we differ in material possessions so do we differ in the vast array of intangible resources that are evident among us. These are those innate abilities that make some of us good singers, for example, while others are tone deaf. Some can paint or sculpt while others can dance or swim. Some have excellent physical health while others have excellent mental health. Some have external, physical beauty while others have beautiful personalities.

Not only do we have different gifts but some of us have many gifts while others have few. We are each unique in the combination of things that make us persons. We all have a common stewardship, however, in that whatever we have is part of who we are, which is in itself a gift of God.

Christians have another important gift from God. This too is part of their lives. It is the gift of the assurance that God loves all persons. This is the gospel or "good news." We are privileged to be given the conviction that God's kingdom of righteousness will come. This belief and hope is an important gift over which we have stewardship.

There is nothing that we possess over which we are not stewards. Each and every one of us in both our individual and corporate relationships are subject to the principle of stewardship with respect to all the tangible and intangible things that we have.

WHAT IS *RESPONSIBLE* STEWARDSHIP?

If we really accept our role as stewards rather than owners then it is apparent that we should use our resources according to the wishes of the owner. Being partners and co-workers with God we will adopt a different *attitude* toward our possessions than if we are treating them as being purely ours to do with as we wish. As wise and responsible stewards, we adopt a caring attitude toward others. We are motivated out of a desire to respond to God's call to be engaged in a great work with him. We use all that we are and possess with concern for others.

In recognition of their responsibilities to God, the Saints have identified four principles of sound stewardship. *Inheritance* applies to all that we are given when we are born into the world and at subsequent times throughout our lives. We spend the years of our lives providing for the basic needs of our families. We use our skills, for example, to earn money with which to buy food, clothing, shelter, and other needed items. But the wise use of our resources enables us to accumulate an *increase* which is above and beyond that which is necessary for our own existence. It is this increase that is available for sharing with others and also for providing ourselves with benefits beyond the basic necessities. Increase is also used to develop long-term security for ourselves—to provide for our future needs over the anticipated duration of our lives.

After these long-term provisions have been made some stewards have *surplus* resources that can be consecrated to the church for its use in various programs of ministry. The accumulated surpluses of material resources, money, skills, and other valuable assets become a *storehouse* which provides resources of ministry to persons in need.

It is easy to see these principles applying to our financial resources, but it is important that they also be seen in terms of time, talent, material possessions, and other resources that we have. Application of the principles of inheritance, increase, surplus, and storehouse is our concrete recognition of God's claim on our lives.

These principles do not deny that God has given us our agency. We *are* free to make choices. As responsible stewards, however, we realize that by accepting God's call we have limited the choices that are available to us. Even though we may theoretically still have the power to squander our resources selfishly, in actual practice this is not an option that we consider. Responsible stewardship is the use of those things over which we have custody in a manner consistent with our understanding of God's love for *all* people. It is living in partnership with God in the achievement of his purposes. We control our own needs in relationship to our understanding of God's love for *all* people. It is living in partnership with God in the achievement of his purposes. We control our own needs in relationship to our understanding of these purposes. We desire to maximize our fruitfulness so that there will be an abundance of our gifts available for the purposes of bringing ministry to other people.

The *financial law* of the church symbolizes the commitment of our entire lives to the purposes of God. The Presiding Bishopric is responsible for interpreting this law and developing procedures for its implementation. They do this as part of their responsibilities carried out under the general administration of the First Presidency who are the chief interpreters of church law. Consistent with the four principles already described, the following procedures are used. Members are encouraged to make an annual accounting. This takes the form of a tithing statement which indicates the member's total income and expenses for "basic living needs" (e.g. food, clothing, shelter, transportation, etc.). Increase is then determined by subtracting the basic living expenses from total income. *Tithing* is computed as one tenth of the *increase.* These procedures permit members to indicate which parts of their incomes are necessary to sustain an adequate standard of living. The rest of their incomes are then available for investments, savings, charitable contributions, extra ("luxury") expenses, etc. Members are encouraged to contribute one-tenth of the increase as tithing to the church to finance its worldwide ministries. Members are also invited to contribute from their increase to the maintenance of the local congregation that they attend and to other charitable causes of their choice.

This method of financial giving is consistent with the necessity to first provide adequately for oneself and family. Remaining resources are available to provide for the needs of others. Saints are encouraged to use their incomes in such a way that they will achieve increase. This is according to the injunction, "Repression of unnecessary wants is in harmony with the law of stewardship and becomes my people" (Doctrine and Covenants 147:5b). It provides opportunity to contribute to the work of the church financially and to save and invest for personal security.

The church provides other opportunities for the use of persons' resources for the benefit of others. Members are invited to contribute to various local and World Church funds that are used for special purposes.

Money is symbolic of and the means toward obtaining material possessions. By financial accounting, we are able to keep track of how we spend our money and buy material possessions. But more important, we are helped to be better managers and to identify ourselves more closely in partnership with God. We also have things that money will not buy. Responsible stewardship reaches beyond money and material goods. It is also important to the consideration of our intangible resources. A good artist cannot achieve consistently without considerable practice. This is true regardless of how much natural ability that artist might possess. Wise stewardship demands the development of our talents. Yet it is not sufficient to develop our talents for our own use exclusively. Many times we have abilities that others do not have. We are responding to God's invitation to be concerned about others when we share what we have with others who are without. Budgeting and accounting procedures can also be applied to the use of our talents. It is important to be just as deliberate and accountable for the use of our intangible resources as we are for our material resources. Wise stewards use what they have intentionally with thought as to consequences and options. The principles of inheritance, increase, surplus, and storehouse are just as applicable to our non-monetary resources as they are to finances.

Another gift that we all have in common is time. Each of us has twenty-four hours in a day. The only difference is that some of us live a greater total number of days than others. We need carefully to plan how our time will be used. We can achieve "increase" with respect to time if we make sure that every moment is not spent frantically doing the things necessary to stay alive. It is important that we have "increase" in time to be with our families and to spend in ministering to the needs of others. It is clear that haphazard, thoughtless use of time does not reflect responsible stewardship.

For some of us, life brings with it sound physical and mental health. Others experience occasional or frequent sickness. Still others are disabled in a variety of ways. Regardless of our circumstances in this regard, our *health* is part of our stewardship. As wise stewards we regard our bodies as instruments for the work of God. Care of the body includes such important concerns as appropriate diet and exercise. The Saints have always been concerned with these matters as evidenced by their abstinence from the use of tobacco and alcoholic beverages. One's health is more than a personal matter. Our families, friends, and colleagues are all affected by the decisions we make about our health. We are responsible for what we eat and drink and for being informed as to the benefits and dangers of various foods, drugs, and other items relating to our health.

Our knowledge that God loves all persons is a gift over which we have custody. What does this mean for us? It really means that we shouldn't keep this gift just for ourselves. The very nature of this gift compels us to share it with others. This, of course, is the meaning of evangelism as discussed in an earlier chapter. We are stewards over this gift that God wishes all people to accept. He has not just given it to a selected few. He would like all persons to recognize Christ as Lord of their lives. The importance of this particular stewardship is made more evident when we remember that we ourselves received this gift and assurance through contact with someone else. This is the way the Christian message is communicated. The responsibility to share it with others is a vital part of our stewardship. If we take our partnership with God seriously the good news becomes part of our lives. We are found continually responding to Jesus' great commission to "go ye therefore, and teach all nations."

Let us return to life itself. How often do we give consideration to where our lives are going? What are our goals? What do we want to accomplish? Are we so caught up in trying to cope with day-to-day situations that there isn't time to reflect on the meaning and direction of our lives? As wise stewards we need to find time for this kind of thought and planning. We need to see our lives as continuous partnerships with God. Short-term decisions must be made with this long-range concern in mind. We need to give purpose and direction to our lives. Our homes, jobs, and the persons with whom we associate must all be chosen deliberately. Our lives are given to us by God. They can be meaningful and fulfilling or they can be empty and without purpose. God makes it possible for us to enjoy good, happy, abundant lives. As responsible stewards we can make the most of this opportunity by giving our lives wholly to fulfilling God's purposes.

OUR CORPORATE STEWARDSHIP

Our discussion of stewardship so far has been almost completely confined to the individual. Yet we do not live alone. We are surrounded by hundreds, thousands, even millions of people. Through the medium of television we are aware of people whom we have never met. Recurrent in our discussion of the individual has been the responsibility God calls us to have for the well-being of other people. This is at the heart of stewardship. Not only are we aware of others but we interact with them in a variety of group settings. Groups, just as much as individuals, have resources at their disposal. They too make decisions as to how these resources are used. Responsible *corporate* stewardship requires that a group use its resources to accomplish the objectives determined by the persons who organized or who are members of the group. This is as true for the church as an organization as it is for any other group. Let us look at some aspects of the church's corporate stewardship.

The church is an intentional accumulation of various kinds of resources directed toward a purpose. There are person resources, material resources, intangible resources, and of course the resource of the Christian message itself. The principles of stewardship earlier described as applying to individuals also apply to the church. God is the owner and founder of the church and has called it into being for a purpose. That purpose is to witness to his saving activity in the world—to witness to Jesus Christ. Responsible stewardship, as far as the church is concerned, means that all the resources of the church are used in ways that contribute to this purpose. The church is responsible for witnessing to the community in which it resides. For this reason it is accountable for its stewardship not just to God and its members but also to the community. The community has a right to expect the church to be active on its behalf.

In carrying out its stewardship the church needs carefully to plan how it will use its resources. It must define its purpose, assess needs, establish goals and objectives, plan strategy, conduct activities, and evaluate its program. It is not sufficient that the church continue "business as usual" without careful thought as to direction and the purposes of God. The church as an institution is steward over all its resources. Above all, it has been called to build the kingdom of God on earth and to witness to the saving power of Jesus Christ. Stewardship over this mission is the church's greatest responsibility.

In 1964 the president of the Saints Church, W. Wallace Smith, included the following in an inspired message to the church: "Stewardship is the response of my people to the ministry of my Son and is required alike of all those who seek to build the kingdom" (Doctrine and Covenants 147:5a). Those who believe firmly that God cares for them and have experienced this assurance in their lives respond to this gift. They use what they have in the service of all persons. This is the meaning of the gospel and this is the responsibility of the disciple.

CHAPTER 17

WHAT IT MEANS TO BE A MEMBER

The foregoing chapters have provided information about the history, belief, organization, and practice of the Saints Church. This book introduces only the main elements and no more than scratches the surface in all but a very few subjects. Even so, the reader who has had little if any previous exposure to these things may have difficulty putting them together in a neat package. This chapter will attempt to pull together that which has been presented previously. However, it cannot present a neatly packaged summary that will be easily understood and readily accepted by all. To do so would be impossible. The full and complete answer to the question "What does it mean to be a member of the Saints Church?" never comes. Persons who have been members of the church for fifty years are still struggling to answer this question. On the other hand, we don't raise our hands in despair. Whatever understanding, meaning, and significance we can grasp will help us along the way. This chapter will summarize briefly the significance of *history*, *belief*, *organization*, and *practice* of the Saints Church and relate it to the life of the member.

THE SIGNIFICANCE OF HISTORY

Written history is the product of looking at yesterday through the eyes of today. History is too often dismissed as irrelevant because it deals with the past. It does deal with the past, but it also deals with the present. We have all heard that those who ignore the past and refuse to learn from its mistakes are condemned to repeat these mistakes. History, then, is important to us for at least two reasons. First, we are today the filter through which the past is seen. Second, we can learn from the past and live more fulfilled lives as a result.

What has been said here about history is not less true for the Saints than it is for any other group of people. The historical overview in Chapter 1 goes back in time only as far as the beginning of the Latter Day Saint movement in the early 1800s. However, the Saints Church has a rich religious and cultural heritage that goes back many centuries. It is important that this be remembered. The continued use of scriptural records written centuries ago is evidence of the importance of this heritage to the present-day life of the church. The Saints Church is where it is today partly because of the struggles and the ambitions of people of former years who sensed the call of God to them. This heritage spans the years from the earliest Old Testment persons through the years of exile, persecution, and redemption of the Hebrew nation. It also covers the life and ministry of Jesus and the formation, struggles, and proliferation into separate groups of the Christian Church up to the religious revivalism of the early nineteenth century and beyond.

The Saints are not isolated from their cultural heritage. The people of God do not live in a vacuum or in isolation from others. They are immersed in the pains and the joys of God's world. The impact of the cultural setting of early nineteenth-century frontier America on the formation and development of the Saints Church is important. This church is what it is today partly as a result of what happened then and what has happened since in the United States and in other countries where the church is located.

Within the life and times of the Saints Church familiar themes are evident. Such themes as persecution, faith, utopian idealism, struggle, failure, success, worldliness, and idolatry are all recurrent in the history of this people. The willingness to accept and embrace the bad as well as the good aspects of their past is a sign of character among peoples. History is significant to a people only to the extent that it is seen as an integral part of who they are today. The Saints are thankful for their past and acknowledge the significance that it has for who they are and who they will become.

THE SIGNIFICANCE OF BELIEF

All people have beliefs. Beliefs are those realities that persons affirm as significant in their lives and on which they base their actions. A community of persons shares many things in common. Religious communities (churches) share common beliefs. Although no two persons believe exactly alike, it is possible to identify certain areas of belief that are shared by all members of a community. This is, of course, true of the Saints Church as it is of other churches. Some areas of common belief have been described earlier in this book. Among the more important are belief in God who reveals himself, Jesus Christ who is our Savior, the worth and dignity of all persons, the call to responsible stewardship, scripture as a record of God's interaction with people, and the call to build Zion.

Beliefs help define the nature of the community. They serve to unite and help people see themselves as members of a group rather than as individuals. Beliefs give a community a sense of identity. They also serve to summarize the bases of the faith and to preserve them for future generations. Beliefs permit persons to affirm together that which they share in common.

Traditionally, churches have been tempted to solidify their beliefs into a written statement called a *creed*. This has its shortcomings because beliefs are the affirmations of the whole person and cannot ever be adequately described in a written statement. However, there are times when it is necessary to write down such statements. They serve useful functions. Statements of belief are used in worship as brief corporate statements of affirmation. They serve to identify the common aspects of our faith at a given point in time. They are also used to tell other persons what is central to the belief of a group of people. Although the Saints Church has avoided the formulation and use of creeds as such, they have used statements of belief. Joseph Smith developed the first such statement of the Latter Day Saint Church in response to an inquiry from the editor of a Chicago newspaper. The statement was later printed in the church periodical and has been used in modified form ever since. On pages 210-215 in the Appendix to this book there appears a recent statement of belief developed by a church committee on basic beliefs. It is the intent of this particular statement to indicate the major, or basic, beliefs of the church. Members are encouraged to think through the beliefs as stated and develop their own interpretations rather than to accept or memorize them as they are printed. A corporate statement of belief cannot be a substitute for one's personal belief. It may be convenient and in some cases appropriate to ask what the church believes on a certain issue. At the same time, the question of belief is, in the final analysis, a personal question.

THE SIGNIFICANCE OF ORGANIZATION

The church is seen as a community of persons with a definite purpose and calling. The church is also an organization, with all the functions, procedures, offices, and other ingredients that are characteristic of all organizations. Chapter 11 briefly described how the Saints Church is organized. Much more could have been written and indeed has been in other publications. Institutions sometimes become so overburdened with organizational details that they cease to function effectively. One principle of sound organization is that "form follows function." This implies that organizational forms serve to carry out functions that are important to the life of the institution. Another implication is that forms, procedures, offices, and structures should be modified or discontinued if they do not contribute to these necessary functions. This requires *flexible* organization.

Even though many organizational forms of the Saints Church are the same or similar now to the way they were over a hundred years ago, some are not. An excellent example is the way the various jurisdictions of the church are organized throughout the world. Every year there are newly organized or reorganized regions, stakes, districts, congregations, branches, and missions in the church. The necessity for flexible structure is affirmed in inspired counsel given to the church by President W. Wallace Smith in 1964:

Instruction which has been given in former years is applicable in principle to the needs of today and should be so regarded by those who are seeking to accomplish the will of their heavenly father. But the demands of a growing church require that these principles should be evaluated and subjected to further interpretation.—Doctrine and Covenants 147:7.

There is a continuous tension between the comfort and familiarity with things as they are on the one hand and the need for change on the other. Organizational patterns are vital to the life of the church. They make the accomplishment of its purpose and objectives possible. The Saints Church accepts this reality and tries to keep its organizational patterns appropriate to its call to be the people of God in today's world.

THE SIGNIFICANCE OF PRACTICE

History, belief, and organization are all important but they tell very little about the life-style of the church. This is what Chapter 12 tried to describe. Even so, there is no way that anyone can really understand and appreciate what a group is like by merely reading a book, no matter how detailed that book may be. One must meet with the Saints in order to find out who they are and what they do. Practice and life-style cannot be adequately described in words. They are, however, as important as the other aspects of the church previously described. What the Saints do from day to day and from week to week defines what the church community is like.

Partly because of their small numbers, the Saints have developed a special sense of community. It is not uncommon to hear one exclaim, "I know I am among the Saints!" This is not a pompous and arrogant claim. It is a recognition that all church members share a common heritage and membership. Frequently when members visit a congregation or branch away from their home they meet people who are acquainted with persons whom they themselves also know. This deepens the sense of closeness that unifies the Saints worldwide. Customarily, members of the church who are not well enough acquainted to be on first-name basis will call each other Brother____ or Sister____, using their last names. This is an important symbol of unity and friendship.

In their life together, the Saints place much emphasis on worship and Christian education. In particular, celebration of the sacraments is an important sense of identity within the church. Together with pastoral care and stewardship ministries, worship and education serve to equip members for the important ministries of outreach. Even though these various functions of the church are generally supported by all active members, there are differences of opinion. The life-style of the church is characterized by many people, with different interests, gifts, and perspectives. Even though it is possible to identify common beliefs and concerns, individuals express and interpret these differently. For the most part, the Saints accept each other's differences in a spirit of toleration, realizing that the church moves forward with the efforts of a variety of persons with different interests and perspectives.

CHAPTER 18

PERSONAL IDENTITY

God's love for persons is not limited. He gives it without reservation because he is the very source of love. Furthermore, God's love is not conditional. He loves us in spite of our misdeeds and misplaced ideals. The gospel presents a message of salvation and hope. It also presents us with a call to respond to God's love. That call is not so much a requirement as an invitation to respond to God's act of reaching out.

Our response takes place in two ways. First, in terms of the world around us, we respond to persons as well as to other parts of our environment. In doing so, we make decisions about our behavior. In general terms, this is called ethics and will be covered in the next chapter.

We also respond in terms of our own personal identity—that is, how are we as persons changed by our encounter with the gospel? In what ways do we feel differently about ourselves? The apostle Paul said, "Therefore, if anyone is in Christ, he is a new creation; the old has passed, behold, the new has come" (II Corinthians 5:17, R.S.V.).

What is this "new creation"? How do we see ourselves as persons in the light of the gospel? First, the gospel opens the possibility of self-acceptance. Most of us seem to have a tendency to be critical of ourselves. We are, very often, not as competent, as articulate, as righteous, or as good-looking as we would like to be. As a result, we may often feel guilty about being less than our ideal selves. Worse yet, we may feel it necessary to pretend to be perfect so that other people will accept us. Thus, we are caught in a trap of pretending to be more competent, articulate, and righteous than we really are. Knowing that we are attempting to deceive others, and fearing exposure of our true selves, we feel even more guilty.

The word of God in Jesus says that we are loved and accepted by God in spite of our shortcomings. Through Jesus Christ, our lives have meaning and significance. There is no longer any need to pretend to be more righteous, confident, knowledgeable, charitable, or good-looking than we really are. We can be open and honest with ourselves and in our relationships with others. There is no longer any need to feel guilty or to fear the judgments of other persons.

Second, the gospel opens to us the possibility of being more aware of who we are as persons. By accepting ourselves, we can look openly at who we are. Thomas Merton, in his book *Contemplation in a World of Action*, speaks of what it means to have an identity. Identity, he says, "means having a belief one stands by; it means having certain definite ways of responding to life, of meeting its demands, of loving other people, and in the last analysis, of serving God. In this sense, identity is one's witness to truth in one's life" (page 78).

". . . a belief one stands by . . ."

We are shaped by the way in which we understand our world. A belief in what is ultimately and finally real is a necessary part of our identity. All of the world's great religions have a belief that its adherents stand by. Even the Marxists have a belief in something ultimate—a historical dynamic known as "dialectical materialism." Even unbelief can be a form of belief if it is "stood by." Our belief tells us something about who we are as persons and how we see ourselves in relation to other persons and things. Our belief provides us with a portion of our identity.

Of course, it is possible to stand by nothing, not even a stance of unbelief. It is possible to live with no integrating perspective about what life is finally about. To do so, however, is to leave a void in our identity. It is also dangerous to move too far in the other direction—that is, we could believe in something so much that we could close ourselves off to any new information or experience. This would be to deny that we are either in need of or capable of growth. Rather, we must establish a belief that we can stand by and defend. At the same time we need to be open enough to listen honestly to the challenges which such a belief encounters in dialogue with others.

"*. . . certain definite ways of responding to life . . .*"

Life has a way of "coming at us." Things happen to us. We each respond to life in our own unique ways. Part of our identity is to be found in the ways we respond to things that happen to us. How do we respond, for example, to a frustrating situation? We could ignore it. We could respond emotionally and strike out (verbally or physically) at the nearest person. Our response should be rational, an attempt to find a logical way to avoid the frustration. Most of us probably respond in a way that combines parts of all of these reactions but no two of us respond in exactly the same way.

How do we respond to love and acceptance shown to us by other persons? We may return that love in an appropriate way. On the other hand, we may be afraid to trust others and attempt to maintain our physical and emotional "distance" from them. Again, our individual responses are unique and may involve various combinations of the alternatives presented here.

Whenever life confronts us, whenever we experience other persons, whenever we take a close look at ourselves, we respond in a way which expresses something of our own personal identity.

Being a Christian means that we respond to life in the light of the gospel. This does not mean that our responses are now the same as everyone else's. It does not mean that we lose our identity. It does mean, however, that it is possible to respond from a particular perspective. We can respond knowing that God loves us. Thus, we have no need to fear life when we are encountered by it. We can also respond in hope, knowing that God is bringing about his kingdom in human history. Thus, we can respond in anticipation of the future.

"*. . . of loving other people . . .*"

What does it mean to love other people? This question is not easily answered, for there is a sense in which it means something different for each of us. We express love in our unique way, and the love of others has its unique impact on each of us.

From the gospel, we can begin to see what it means for us to love other people. Through the crucifixion and resurrection of Jesus Christ, we learn that to love others is to give one's self for them. Thus, loving others is not first of all a means of satisfying our own needs for affection and acceptance. Rather, it is a giving of ourselves to other people.

Yet this kind of love is not possible unless we know and accept ourselves. We must have an honest view of our own identity. Otherwise, we may be inclined to feed our own egos under the pretense of loving others. This creates problems. First, we can mislead ourselves by believing that we are loving others while, in fact, serving our own interests. Second, we can come into conflict with others because we are using rather than serving them. Of course, we usually find ourselves somewhere between loving others completely and serving only ourselves. We are usually neither as loving nor as self-serving as we could be. Thus, it is something we must be continually working with. We must struggle to know ourselves better while, at the same time, trying to express our love more fully.

Our love for others is not something which should be passed over lightly, for love is the vehicle by which we grow closer to God. Because we are unique persons, the love of each of us for others is a separate gift. No one else can give the love which I myself can give, for it is an expression of my identity. My love for others cannot be separated from who I am as a person.

". . . of serving God . . ."

In a very similar vein, no one else can give our service to God. But just what is service to God? Jesus said, "Truly, I say to you, as you did it to one of the least of these my brethren, you did it to me" (Matt. 25:40, R.S.V.). A similar thought is expressed by the prophet Micah, who said, "And what does the Lord require of you but to do justice, and to love kindness, and to walk humbly with your God?" (Micah 6:8, R.S.V.). The Book of Mormon presents a similar understanding in the words "When you are in the service of your fellow beings you are only in the service of your God" (Mosiah 1:49).

Self-giving love requires that we know who we are. It requires that we do justice, love kindness, and walk humbly with God. It demands that we treat every person as though he or she were the Christ. Serving God occurs in the self-giving love of those who follow the Christ.

"...one's witness to truth in one's life..."

Our personal identity, that unique combination of personal qualities which is just "me" and "you," is more than just a way of distinguishing one person from another. It is one's witness to truth in one's life.

As soon as we are born, we begin to evaluate our experience of life. We begin to make decisions about what we believe to be true. Our identity reflects the truth that we perceive. It witnesses to the truth we perceive in loving others, in serving God, in responding to life. Who we are witnesses to the truth we stand by.

DEVOTION

Our identity is closely related to the truth to which we witness. Therefore, it is important to become aware of who we are and the truth to which we are witnessing. Very often in our society, we seem to spend all of our time running here and there. We spend so much time doing things that we lose sight of our ultimate intentions.

There is a need, then, for time to reflect on who we are and who we wish to be. We have a need to make conscious decisions about the truth to which our lives will witness. This need has been met by what the church has called devotions, or prayer and meditation. Prayer is an intense probing of our souls in the presence of God. It is our attempt to give expression to our aspirations, intentions, feelings, and beliefs. To pray is to become aware of ourselves in relation to God. It is to express doubt as well as faith. It is to confess who we have been and who we intend to become.

In a society which values activity and "getting things done," it is becoming more important to spend some time alone, "doing" nothing. This is so that we can come to terms with who we are and who we wish to become. Because we profess to be Christians, this reflection naturally takes place in the light of the Word which God has given us in Jesus Christ. In any case, being Christian has an important impact on who we are as persons and how we see ourselves. Therefore, it is important that we take the time to look honestly at ourselves so that we can determine what that impact will be.

Identity then is rooted in our conviction that God loves us. We never cease to struggle with the question of who we are and what our role in society is. However, we can at the same time experience the peace that only faith in God can bring. The assurance that we are his sons and daughters brings hope and joy into our lives.

CHAPTER 19

ETHICS: DECISIONS, DECISIONS, DECISIONS

We become Christian to be more effectively engaged in life, not to escape from it. Engagement in life means being constantly faced with the necessity of making decisions. Each day we make literally thousands of decisions. Some are inconsequential: What will I wear today? What shall I have for breakfast? Other decisions may be quite significant and may have major impact on the future of our lives: Should I begin a new career? Should I get married? Should we have another child?

We might ask ourselves how to make decisions and what factors to consider before making them. When we ask these kinds of questions, we are asking about ethics. Ethics has to do with how we make decisions about how to act in relation to the world around us. It deals with what we decide is the "right" and the "wrong" thing to do. Our ethics determine how we will relate to persons as well as to the physical world.

In our society today, ethics can be a problem. Finding a sound basis on which to make decisions is becoming very difficult for many people. It used to be that ethical principles were generally agreed upon by most persons in society. Very often churches have had much influence. The Scriptures and the church's teachings have had wide acceptance. Thus persons were able to make their decisions on the basis of widely accepted principles. For those who accepted the situation—and most did—right and wrong were clearly defined.

Today, however, we are faced with a different situation. Within some very loose restrictions imposed by the law, persons are free to make whatever decisions they choose. We live in the midst of a "new morality" in which for some of us right and wrong are largely matters of personal preference. Ethical principles proclaimed by institutions such as the church seem to be less and less meaningful to many persons. Absolute moral codes covering every aspect of life no longer seem to be of interest to people in our society. This is especially true when we are confronted with "new" ethical dilemmas such as genetic manipulation and the possibility of nuclear war.

What are we to make of this situation? Is it no longer possible to make "ethical" decisions? Are there fewer and fewer ethical persons these days? What does it mean for us to be ethical in our decision-making today? The answers do not come easily. Perhaps we can approach these questions by looking at various ways of making ethical decisions.

RULES

For many people, ethics and morality mean rules and laws. This is understandable since the Jewish and Christian traditions have tended to look to various sets of rules and laws for guidance. The Ten Commandments and the Sermon on the Mount are collections of ethical principles which Christians have looked to since the earliest days of the church. They are "in our bones." Many persons in the church find these two sets of rules, along with others in the Scriptures, to be of great help in making ethical decisions.

Still, there are many persons for whom sets of rules do not seem to be adequate. Sometimes rules can be confining rather than liberating. At other times, rules may not be relevant to a particular situation. At still other times, we may be forced to make a decision between two "rights" or between two "wrongs."

We must remember that the ethical admonitions in the Scriptures were given at particular times and to particular groups of people. This is not to say that ethics are completely relative, but we must realize that the ethical rules presented in Scripture are not always to be followed blindly. For example, in the book of Exodus, we are confronted with the following admonition: "Six days shall work be done, but the seventh day is a sabbath of solemn rest, holy to the Lord; whoever does any work on the sabbath day shall be put to death" (31:15, R.S.V.). Few of us would suggest today that working on the sabbath is an activity deserving capital punishment. We do not feel that this rule should be taken literally.

This is not to suggest that sets of rules have no validity for us. They serve a very important function. They summarize general ethical principles and have been helpful to the church through the centuries as it has attempted to understand its ethical responsibilities. They can never be so final that they can tell us exactly what to do in every situation we encounter. But they can be useful as general guidelines. It is important, however, that we understand the times in which they were originally presented and the people to whom they were addressed.

These sets of rules also remind us that there is a sense in which we are obligated to God. He has given us all that we have, even life itself. It is only natural that we should feel a sense of obligation to him in our decision-making. Yet this must be balanced by the gospel's reminder that God loves us even if we do not always "Follow the rules." God's love for us does not depend on our ability to make the right decisions all of the time. This knowledge that we are unconditionally accepted must always be considered alongside our obligation to do God's will. Furthermore, with the passage of time we grow in our understanding of what God requires of us as his disciples.

GOOD SENSE

Another way of looking at ethics is to say that it simply involves using good sense. This approach assumes that rules are not simply arbitrary. There is a *reason* for each ethical rule, and the reason is the most important element in the rule. For example, the Bible says "Thou shalt not kill." One reason for this commandment is that a great deal of social disorganization and personal despair would occur if people went around indiscriminately killing each other.

Ethical rules, then, have a purpose which can be discovered by using our mental faculties. In fact, in this view, reason is at the heart of ethics. Making ethical decisions is a process of using our reason or good sense to determine the best alternative among those that are available to us. If our reasoning is sound, our decisions will probably be right.

Unfortunately, "good sense" is not always as obvious as we might like it to be. Sometimes our situations become very complex. The kinds of things which need to be considered become so numerous or conflicting that it is very difficult to say just what "good sense" or "sound reasoning" might be in some situations.

Another problem is that it is sometimes difficult to tell which decisions are made on the basis of good sense and which are made on the basis of what we really want. Sound reasoning is ideally objective. It should be based solely on facts, but it is very difficult to keep our feelings from influencing our decisions. This is not necessarily bad. At times our feelings are more reliable than our good sense. Still, we should not confuse the situation by saying that our decisions are based on sound reasoning when, in fact, our feelings have a very strong influence.

This approach to ethics does have its strong points, however. It implies that we are all confronted with the necessity of making ethical decisions. We all have the tools of ethical decision-making within us and we are therefore responsible for the decisions we make. Finally, it implies that there is a sound basis for decision-making which makes ethics more than a matter of personal preference.

RELATIONSHIPS

A third way of looking at ethics focuses on persons and relationships. This approach attempts to examine each situation afresh and to make a decision which seems to be appropriate in light of the gospel. The gospel is the good news about God's love for human beings. It says that persons are of great worth in the sight of God. Therefore, our relationships and our decisions should reflect these truths.

The ethical question from this approach, then, is not "What is right according to the rules?" or "What seems to be the most logical decision?" Rather it is "What decision reflects the love of God in this context?" Thus, ethical decisions should reflect the worth of every person. Ethics becomes the practice of developing relationships with others which are meaningful and fulfilling.

This approach sees persons as more important than rules. Rules are intended to be guidelines. They give an indication of the kinds of behavior which are enriching and fulfilling for persons. Yet they are not as important as the persons they are intended to serve. In other words, it is the intention of this approach to discern and carry out the "spirit" of the law as opposed to the "letter" of the law. Each decision is examined on its own merits, and the alternative which seems to be most in keeping with God's intentions for persons is the one which is preferred. In this way, ethics is closely related to the gospel, and cultural factors are not confused with the ethical demands of the gospel.

There are potential problems in this approach, as there are in the others. Viewing each situation afresh can mean that the historical element is ignored. The old saying that "history repeats itself" can become more true than we would like it to be. We may be inclined to confuse our own feelings and wishes with the demands of the gospel.

WHICH APPROACH?

As we have seen, each of these ways of looking at ethics has its advantages and disadvantages. Which one, then, should we use? The answer is that we should be aware of all of them. We should understand that there are several ways in which ethics can be approached from the viewpoint of the gospel. If we are aware of the advantages and pitfalls of each approach, we may be able to make better decisions. Also, by being aware of several approaches to making ethical decisions, we can be more sure that all of the available information is being considered.

Yet we must realize that all of our ethical decisions are subject to error. No matter how hard we try, we cannot be right all of the time. We must make the best decisions possible and trust that God will forgive us for our mistakes.

SOME GENERAL PRINCIPLES

The Saints Church has tended to emphasize certain ethical principles. These must be viewed in the context of the various approaches described. They have been helpful in guiding decision-making by individuals and by the church.

1. *Each person has a special worth and uniqueness in the sight of God.* This is the core of ethical belief. It is rooted in the very heart of the gospel. It serves to remind us that no matter how right we think we are, we must treat persons who believe differently than we do as persons who are loved by God. The worth of persons in the sight of God is a fundamental ethical principle.

2. *Our personal ethics should be such that they allow us to serve God as fully as possible.* One statement supporting this affirmation was delivered to the church by Joseph Smith in 1833. It is included as Section 86 in the Doctrine and Covenants. This "Word of Wisdom" counsels persons to see that their personal behavior does not detract from their physical well-being. It suggests that we should eat wisely and rest adequately. It suggests that the abuse of substances such as alcohol and tobacco may impair our health to the point where we are less able to serve God. The intention of the document is not to provide a basis for judging the behavior of others. Rather, it is

intended to be what it ways it is, a word of wisdom. A more recent position, taken by the World Conference in 1970, states:

> *Resolved,* That it is the conviction of the church that as stewards over their temporal resources, bodies, skills, time, and social influence, it is incumbent upon members of the church to conduct themselves at all times in such manner that they use their resources constructively, promote personal health and well-being, cultivate productive skills, participate in wholesome leisure time activities, and exert an affirmative influence on their fellowmen for their mutual spiritual development and abundant life; and, be it further
>
> *Resolved,* That in making such choices the Saints are admonished to avoid experimentation with or addiction to any activity or habit which is known to have an adverse effect upon health and to avoid conduct which is likely to lead others by either word or example into such activity; and, be it further
>
> *Resolved,* That the conduct of the Saints of all ages in relations between the sexes should be controlled by the principle in the marriage covenant that both spouses will keep themselves "wholly for each other, and from all others" during their lives; and be it further
>
> *Resolved,* That the world fellowship of the Saints, encompassing cultures where different sets of values prevail in respect to the same or similar activities, involving factors sometimes beyond the scope of knowledge and experience of persons not in the same culture, requires the Saints to refrain from passing unrighteous judgment on the conduct of members of the church in other cultures, while each one brings his own life under discipline according to the doctrine of the church and through response to the Holy Spirit.—Resolution 1085.

3. In keeping with the belief in Zion, *our participation in the social order should be directed toward building a society of peace, justice, and personal fulfillment for all persons.* Ethics is not simply a matter of personal behavior. It must inevitably touch the society in which we live. While we are individual persons in our own right, we are also persons who live in community with others. The societies in which we reside should enable persons to live rich and meaningful lives. This ethical imperative should have something to say about our personal decision-making.

Ethics is primarily a matter of free and grateful response to God for his gift to us in Jesus Christ. The heart of ethics is in the gospel. To be ethically responsible is to be in the midst of a tension. On one hand, we are obligated to God for all that he has given us. On the other hand, we have been set free by the salvation we have been given in Jesus Christ. Our understanding of and response to the goal of ethics allows us to be both obedient and free. Such a goal can be met only through the grace of God.

CHAPTER 20

THE SAINTS CHURCH, THE RELIGIOUS COMMUNITY AND THE WORLD

The Saints Church lives under the imperatives laid on it by God. It affirms that God called it into existence and continues to direct its affairs. The Saints believe that they are commissioned and empowered to build God's kingdom in this world. They recognize, however, that they do not live in isolation. The church exists alongside other denominations in the Christian community and alongside other religious institutions in the broader religious community. It also exists in the world. This chapter will explore these two relationships.

THE CHURCH AND THE RELIGIOUS COMMUNITY

There are several hundred separate and distinct churches claiming to authentically represent Jesus Christ in the world. There are many more religious institutions claiming belief in some form of God. This appears to represent a rather confusing situation. Over the years some of these institutions have attempted to dispute the claims of others in an effort to add credibility to their own claims. The fact that one particular organization believes it has been called to be God's agent in the world does not, however, mean that others have not also been called. The Saints Church was reminded of this in an inspired message presented by Elbert A. Smith which said, "I have many forces at work in the world, saith the Lord. I have many spiritual forces at work that you know not of. You see but the smaller part of my work, and the world perceives it not at all" (*Saints' Herald*, Volume 64, No. 46, November 14, 1917).

The Saints, then, believe that they are part of an important work. They affirm the uniqueness of their calling and of the resources which they bring to it. They exist to make God's kingdom a reality in a world of need and believe that God has specifically charged them with this responsibility. Furthermore, they represent a living witness to God's action in the world today. This action is seen in the lives and accomplishments of the Saints. But it is also seen in the efforts of other persons who open their lives to God's influence. Other religious organizations and so called "secular" organizations are also seen as agents of God's redemptive ministries.

The ecumenical movement has been a subject of much discussion among persons interested in organized religion. Ecumenism can be defined in terms of the desires of some to combine several or all churches into one worldwide Christian church. The Saints have never participated in this kind of movement. They do not see their church as merging with others. They intend to retain their identity as a separate denomination.

Ecumenism can also be seen as several churches cooperating on certain of their endeavors. This involves the pooling of some resources on local, national, or international levels. It also includes consultation between representatives of various churches for the purpose of improving effectiveness of their individual tasks. In this sense, the Saints Church does participate in the ecumenical movement. An example of this is participation by headquarters personnel in the National Council of Churches' (U.S.A.) Commission on Stewardship. Although the Saints Church is not a member of the N.C.C. (U.S.A.) this relationship has been mutually beneficial to the Saints Church and the other denominations which have participated. Another example is that of local personnel serving as members of Ministerial Alliance groups in which ministers of several denominations meet together to consider the needs of their community. Yet another example is the invitation of ministers and lay persons from other denominations to speak to classes or preach sermons in the church. Cosponsorship of community services for such special occasions as World Day of Prayer or Good Friday is another example.

Realizing that the task before them is of gigantic proportions, the Saints are interested in reaping all the benefits available from communication and cooperation with other denominations. They see such relationships as significantly enriching their lives as individuals and as an organization. In addition, these relationships enhance the building of God's kingdom.

THE CHURCH AND MORMONISM

The Saints Church is one of at least twenty separate organizations stemming from the original organization of the church in 1830. The two major organizations are the Saints Church and the Church of Jesus Christ of Latter-day Saints, usually called *Mormons.* The Mormon church, with headquarters in Salt Lake City, Utah, is by far the largest with over three million members. Most of the remaining organizations were formed by persons leaving one of the major groups because of doctrinal differences. For the most part they have very small memberships.

The Mormon church and Saints Church became separate organizations during the years following the martyrdom of Joseph Smith in 1844. The two churches differ in significant ways, particularly with respect to belief in the afterlife. Mormons believe in a plurality of gods and in the potential for human beings to become gods themselves. They also practice baptism and other ordinances on behalf of dead persons and believe that marriage can be contracted not only for the present life but for eternity.

On the other hand there are similarities between the two churches. Both use the Book of Mormon and believe in modern-day revelation and scripture. The priesthood structure is similar but with some important differences in responsibility and method of selection. Both churches believe that Zion is the tangible expression of God's kingdom on earth. They each trace their origin to the prophet Joseph Smith and hold him in high esteem.

Differences between the two churches account for what might be described as a traditional rivalry. For many years the Saints Church adopted a defensive posture out of which members attempted to explain to the world how and why they were not "Mormons." This tended to center on the Saints' contention that Joseph Smith had nothing to do with originating the practice of polygamy which was openly practiced by the Mormons in Utah. The Saints' defensive stance can also be explained in part by the fact that they have always been much smaller in numbers than the Mormons.

The Mormon church on the other hand has traditionally denied that the Saints constitute an authoritative extension of the church founded by Joseph Smith. In fact, many Mormons are surprised to find that such an organization as the Saints Church even exists.

In recent years, however, these two churches have taken a more positive stance toward each other. There is, at least to some degree, mutual respect for each other's existence. There are even evidences of cooperation between the two such as in the restoration of historic properties in Nauvoo, Illinois, and the exchange of copies of important early church documents. The Saints Church increasingly tends to see itself in terms of what it *is* rather than what it is not. The Saints Church looks optimistically to the development of more open communication with the Mormons and to the further elimination of barriers to mutual understanding.

This should not be construed to suggest that the basic differences between the two churches are being reduced or eliminated. Nor does it prophesy a reunification of the two churches. The basic differences in doctrine and practice seem to suggest that they will remain as separate organizations in the foreseeable future.

THE CHURCH AND THE WORLD

We have affirmed that the church is called by God to assist in his purpose of redeeming the world and all that is in it. As Christians we cannot look on as spectators, hoping that God will accomplish his purposes without it being necessary for us to be involved. If we are to be the body of Christ we must be immersed in the needs of the world as he was. We must accept responsibility for assisting in the bringing into existence of God's kingdom.

But the Christian Church has not always taken this view. For some, the call to be disciples has been interpreted as a demand that we keep ourselves apart from the world; any association with the evils of the world might make us less able to do God's will ourselves. This view has been expressed in various ways. There are persons who isolate themselves from everyone else as much is humanly possible. This is the position of the hermit. Others choose their associations with the world with great care so as to come in contact only with good things and good people.

It is true that we all need times to be alone. We also need to be aware that certain associations may cause us to become distracted from our call to be disciples of Jesus Christ. Yet isolation from the evils of the world can never bring about their change. A willingness to risk ourselves by becoming involved in the world is necessary if we are to assist God in his work.

As described in earlier chapters, the Saints have always claimed the world as the arena of God's action. They believe that this is where his kingdom will be established. They see themselves as Christ's disciples in all of their relationships. The Saints are aware of the opportunities to witness for him in their day-to-day lives. They know that following him demands their *whole* attention *all* of the time. They are anxiously engaged in the work of building God's kingdom on earth.

This basic stance toward the world enables the Saints to see individuals and organizations of society as potential partners in God's work. Our communities are rich with resources that are available for involvement in God's work. Businesses, government agencies, and community service organizations all represent possibilities for cooperative endeavor between the church and nonreligious groups. The church does not arrogantly march in to change the world. Instead it works with the world in making our communities better places to live. The world can and will become the kind of place where people live in harmony with each other and in the assurance that they are loved by God.

AN INVITATION

As specifically stated in the Preface, this book is designed to be informational. Yet there is much that has been omitted in the interests of brevity. Readers who would like more information on any of the subjects introduced in this book are invited to follow one or more of these procedures:

1. In the appendix to this book (beginning on page 216), there is a list of additional books and resources. These materials may be helpful in exploring the subjects introduced in this book.

2. Those who have questions are invited to write to the church headquarters for additional information. Please write to:

Office of Public Information
Saints Auditorium
Box 1059
Independence, Missouri 64051

3. Anyone is welcome to visit one of the hundreds of branches and congregations of the church throughout the world. The maps on pages 120-121 show where the larger concentrations of members are found. More specific information on location of churches and the

names of local representatives can be obtained by writing to the church's public information office at the address listed above. Many names, addresses, and phone numbers are listed in telephone directories. Look for the full name of the church (Reorganized Church of Jesus Christ of Latter Day Saints) in the yellow pages or white pages.

The authors of this book would like to issue more than an invitation to seek additional information. Each of us is actively involved in the ministries of the Saints Church because we firmly believe that God has called this church to an important work. We would like to extend to everyone the invitation to witness for Christ and to build God's kingdom on earth. We believe that much can and will be accomplished as persons work together with God in the accomplishment of his purposes. Won't you join with the Saints and experience the satisfaction of meaningful service to God and your fellow beings? The invitation is freely extended to all.

APPENDIX

STATEMENT OF FAITH AND BELIEF OF THE SAINTS CHURCH

1. We believe in God the eternal Father, source and center of all love and life and truth, who is almighty, infinite, and unchanging, in whom and through whom all things exist and have their being.
2. We believe in Jesus Christ, the Only Begotten Son of God, who is from everlasting to everlasting; through whom all things were made; who is God in the flesh, being incarnate by the Holy Spirit for man's salvation; who was crucified, died, and rose again; who is mediator between God and man, and the judge of both the living and the dead; whose dominion has no end.
3. We believe in the Holy Spirit, the living presence of the Father and the Son, who in power, intelligence, and love works in the minds and hearts of men to free them from sin, uniting them with God as his sons, and with each other as brethren. The Spirit bears record of the Father and of the Son, which Father, Son, and Holy Ghost are one God.
4. We believe that the Holy Spirit empowers men committed to Christ with gifts of worship and ministry. Such gifts, in their richness and diversity, are divided severally as God wills, edifying the body of Christ, empowering men to encounter victoriously the circumstances of their discipleship, and confirming the new creation into which men are called as sons of God.

5. We believe that the Holy Spirit creates, quickens, and renews in men such graces as love, joy, peace, mercy, gentleness, meekness, forbearance, temperance, purity of heart, brotherly kindness, patience in tribulation, and faithfulness before God in seeking to build up his kingdom.

6. We believe that man is endowed with freedom and created to know God, to love and serve him, and enjoy his fellowship. In following the dictates of pride and in declaring his independence from God, man loses the power to fulfill the purpose of his creation and becomes the servant of sin, whereby he is divided within himself and estranged from God and his fellows. This condition, experienced by our ancestors who first came to a knowledge of good and evil, is shared by all who are granted the gift of accountability.

7. We believe that man cannot be saved in the kingdom of God except by the grace of the Lord Jesus Christ, who loves us while we are yet in our sins, and who gave his life to reconcile us unto God. Through this atonement of the Lord Jesus Christ and by the gift of the Holy Spirit, men receive power to choose God and to commit their lives to him; thus are they turned from rebellion, healed from sin, renewed in spirit, and transformed after the image of God in righteousness and holiness.

8. We believe that all men are called to have faith in God and to follow Jesus Christ as Lord, worshiping the Father in his name. In this life those who hear the gospel and repent should commit their lives to Christ in baptism by immersion in water and the laying on of hands. Through living by these principles they participate in God's promise of forgiveness, reconciliation, and eternal life.

9. We believe that the church was established by Jesus Christ. In its larger sense it encompasses those both living and dead who, moved by the Spirit of God, acknowledge Jesus as Lord. In its corporate sense, it is

the community of those who have covenanted with Christ. As the body of Christ through which the Word of God is tangibly expressed among men, the church seeks to discern the will of God and to surrender itself to him in worship and service. It is enlightened, sustained, and renewed by the Holy Spirit. It is to bring the good news of God's love to all people, reconciling them to God through faith in Jesus Christ. The church administers the ordinances through which the covenant is established, cares for all within its fellowship, ministers to the needy, wages war on evil, and strives for the kingdom of God.

10. We believe that all men are called to be stewards under God. They are accountable to him, in the measure of their perception of the divine purpose in creation and redemption, for managing all gifts and resources given into their care. In the exercise of stewardship, men embody the divine will and grow in spiritual maturity through developing native powers and skills achieving dominion over the physical order and perfecting human relationships in the Spirit of Christ.

11. We believe that the kingdom of God sustains men as the stable and enduring reality of history, signifying the total Lordship of God over all human life and endeavor. The kingdom is always at hand in judgment and promise, confronting men with the joyful proclamation of God's rule and laying claim upon them as they acknowledge the new Creation in Christ. The full revelation of the kingdom awaits the final victory over evil, when the will of God shall prevail and his rule shall extend over all human relations to establish the dominion of peace, justice, and truth. To this end the church proclaims the gospel of the kingdom both as present reality and future hope in the midst of a faithless world.

12. We believe that Zion is the means by which the prophetic church participates in the world to embody

the divine intent for all personal and social relations. Zion is the implementation of those principles, processes, and relationships which give concrete expression to the power of the kingdom of God in the world. It affirms the concern of the gospel with the structures of our common life together and promotes the expression of God's reconciling love in the world, thus bringing forth the divine life in human society. The church is called to gather her covenant people into signal communities where they live out the will of God in the total life of society. While this concrete expression of the kingdom of God must have a central point of beginning it reaches out to every part of the world where the prophetic church is in mission.

13. We believe that all are called according to the gifts of God unto them to accept the commission and cost of discipleship. Some are chosen through the spirit of wisdom and revelation and ordained by those who are in authority in the church to serve in specialized ministries. These include ministry to persons, families, and community, as well as preaching, teaching, administering the ordinances, and directing the affairs of the church. The authority of every member of the body in his respective calling emerges out of divine endowment to him and his faithfulness in servanthood with Christ.

14. We believe that the ordinances witness the continuing life of Christ in the church, providing the experiences in which God and man meet in the sealing of covenant. In the ordinances God uses common things, even the nature of man, to express the transcendent and sacramental meaning of creation. God thereby provides the continuing means of investing his grace in human life for its renewal and redemption.

15. We believe that God reveals himself to man. He enters into the minds of men through the Holy Spirit to disclose himself to them and to open their understanding to the

inner meaning of his revelation in history and in the physical order. Revelation centers in Jesus Christ, the incarnate word, who is the ultimate disclosure of truth and the standard by which all other claims to truth are measured.

16. We believe that the Scriptures witness to God's redemptive action in history and to man's response to that action. When studied through the light of the Holy Spirit they illumine men's minds and hearts and empower them to understand in greater depth the revelation in Christ. Such disclosure is experienced in the hearts of men rather than in the words by which the revelation is interpreted and communicated. The Scriptures are open because God's redemptive work is eternal, and our discernment of it is never complete.

17. We believe in the resurrection. This principle encompasses the divine purpose to conserve and renew life. It guarantees that righteousness will prevail and that, by the power of God, men move from death into life. In resurrection God quickens and transforms the soul, i.e. the body and spirit, bringing man into fellowship with his Son.

18. We believe in eternal judgment. It is the wisdom of God bringing the whole creation under divine judgment for good. This judgment is exercised through men as they are quickened by the Holy Spirit to comprehend the eternal implications of divine truth. Through the judgment of God the eternal destiny of men is determined according to divine wisdom and love and according to their response to God's call to them. The principle of eternal judgment acknowledges that Christ is the judge of all human aspiration and achievement and that he summons men to express the truth in decision until all things are reconciled under God.

19. We believe that the inner meaning and end toward which all history moves is revealed in Christ. He is at work in the midst of history, reconciling all things unto

God in order, beauty, and peace. This reconciliation brings to fulfillment the kingdom of God upon earth. Christ's presence guarantees the victory of righteousness and peace over the injustice, suffering, and sin of our world. The tension between our assurance that the victory has been won in Christ and our continuing experience in this world where God's sovereignty is largely hidden is resolved in the conviction that Christ will come again. The affirmation of his coming redeems us from futility and declares the seriousness of all life under the unfailing and ultimate sovereignty of God.

—Reprinted from *Exploring the Faith*,
a series of studies prepared by a
committee on basic beliefs

ADDITIONAL SOURCES

A. HISTORY (Chapter 1)

1. *The History of the Reorganized Church of Jesus Christ of Latter Day Saints*, 8 volumes, Herald House 1951-1976. This is the official history of the church.

B. BASIC CHRISTIAN BELIEF (Chapters 2-4)

1. *Exploring the Faith* by a Committee on Basic Beliefs, Herald House, 1970. This book contains a discussion of each of the statements of faith and belief found on pages 210-215 of this book.
2. *The Theological Enterprise* by Vernone Sparkes, Herald House, 1969. This book introduces theology as a process and includes most of the subjects normally included in this discipline.

C. REVELATION AND SCRIPTURE (Chapters 5-8)

1. The Holy Scriptures, Herald House, latest edition, 1974. This is the Inspired Version of the Bible printed from manuscripts prepared by Joseph Smith.
2. The Book of Mormon, Herald House, 1966 edition.
3. Doctrine and Covenants, Herald House, 1970 edition plus additions. This includes inspired documents presented to the church by its presidents.
4. *The Burning Bush* by Geoffrey Spencer, Herald House, 1974. This book discusses the nature of revelation and Scripture and their role in the church. It briefly introduces each of the three books of Scripture.

5. *Restoration Scriptures: A Study of Their Textual Development* by Richard Howard, Herald House, 1969. This is a somewhat technical discussion of the development of the three standard books.
6. *Scriptures from Ancient America* by Roy Cheville, Herald House, 1964. This book gives some background to the Book of Mormon and provides an overview of its content.
7. *The Book of Mormon Speaks for Itself* by Roy Cheville, Herald House, 1971. This book relates the Book of Mormon message to life today.
8. *Treasure in Earthen Vessels* by William Russell, Herald House, 1965, Independence Press, 1973. This is an overview of the background and content of the New Testament.
9. *Exploring the Faith* (see B. 1 above).
10. *Commentary on the Book of Mormon* by Chris Hartshorn, Herald House, 1964.
11. *Joseph Smith's "New Translation" of the Bible* by Paul Wellington, Herald House, 1970. This is a parallel column comparison of the Inspired and King James versions of the Bible. It includes all verses in which the two versions differ as well as three introductory essays on the Inspired Version.

D. CHURCH PURPOSE, ORGANIZATION, AND PRACTICE (Chapters 9-12)

1. *The Body of Christ* by Harold Schneebeck, Herald House, 1968. This book describes the nature and purpose of the church.
2. *For What Purpose Assembled* by Donald Landon and Robert Smith, Herald House, 1969, Independence Press, 1973. This book describes the functioning of the local congregation.
3. *Exploring the Faith* (see B. 1 above).
4. *Congregational Leaders Handbook*, Herald House, published annually. This briefly explains the six

functions of congregational life and provides themes for each unit in the church year.

5. *Handbook of Church Organization and Administrative Policies and Procedures* by the First Presidency, Herald House, 1974. This is a comprehensive statement of church organization and procedure.
6. *Resources for Women's Ministries* by Women's Ministries Commission, Herald House, 1975. This outlines various models of church organization with emphasis on possibilities for women in the church.
7. *The Priesthood Manual* by Alfred Yale, Herald House, 1972 edition. This outlines the various functions and responsibilities of priesthood.
8. *Called and Sent* by Loyd Adams and others, Herald House, 1972. This explains the various functions of congregational life.
9. *Pastoral Care: The Fruit of the Spirit* by Dan Fenn and Peter Judd, Herald House, 1975. This explores the role of pastoral care in the church.
10. *The Church and Its Mission* by Paul Booth, Herald House, 1971. This explores the overall mission of the church.

E. EVANGELISM AND THE KINGDOM OF GOD (Chapters 13-15)

1. *Readings on Concepts of Zion*, edited by Paul Wellington, Herald House, 1973. A collection of readings providing varying views on Zionic theory and practice.
2. *Exploring the Faith* (see B. 1 above).
3. *Evangelism: The Spirit of Community* by James Cable, Mary Jowett, Peter Judd, and Joe Serig, Herald House, 1974. This book explores the nature of evangelism.
4. *Called and Sent* (see D. 8 above).

F. STEWARDSHIP (Chapter 16)

1. *The Response of My People*, seminar kit prepared by the Christian Education Office, Herald House, 1972. This is a collection of papers and other resources relating to the principle of stewardship.
2. *In the Manner Designed of God*, *Money Management Matters*, *Tips on Inheritance Planning for Stewards*, and *Response and Account Ability*, by the Presiding Bishopric, 1971-1975. A series of four booklets on various aspects of stewardship with emphasis on finances.
3. *Exploring the Faith* (see B. 1 above).
4. *Called and Sent* (see D. 8 above).
5. *Stewardship: The Response of My People* by Nancy Tanner Edwards and Peter A. Judd, Herald House, 1976. This book explores the nature of stewardship through the use of a variety of educational and worship activities.

All publications listed are currently (October 1975) in print and are available from Herald House, Drawer HH, Independence, Missouri 64055. Call 800-821-7550 (toll free) to order or for information on prices.

INDEX

Note: An attempt has been made to include in this index all the major concerns covered in this book. The index also includes key names and places. The reader is advised to follow the discussion of the issue to its completion in the book which will often carry over to pages following those listed in the index.

A

Administration — 115
Administration to the Sick — 112
Administrative Services — 124
Apocrypha — 73
Apostasy — 100
Apostle — 107, 115, 126
Appointees — 126
Audio-Visual — 124
Authority — 67

B

Baptism — 101, 110, 112
Basic Beliefs Committee — 125

Belief — 180, 182, 210
Bible — 13, 65, 71, 72, 91, 133
Bishop — 107, 117, 122, 126, 171
Blessing of Children — 111
Body of Christ — 93, 103, 114, 140
Bondage — 45
Book of Mormon — 13, 17, 20, 65, 71, 83, 90, 91, 133, 140, 204
Branch — 107, 118, 122, 129, 182
Briggs, Jason — 24
Broadcasting — 124

C

Calling — 93, 103, 213
Campus Ministry — 124
Canonization — 67, 73
Center Place — 20, 160
Chosen — 93
Claims — 15, 21
Communications — 124
Conference — 25, 26
Confession — 46
Confirmation — 110
Congregation — 107, 116, 129, 182
Countries — 121
Covenant — 101, 110, 114
Cowdery, Oliver — 19
Creation — 36, 41, 58
Crucifixion — 49

D

Deacon — 106

Death — 42
Decisions — 192
Devotion — 190
Dispersion — 23
Distinguishing Characteristics — 12
District — 107, 118, 129, 182
Divine — 48
Doctrine and Covenants — 13, 65, 71, 88, 107, 129, 133

E

Early Church — 19
Ecumenical — 201
Education — 28, 96, 105, 124, 134, 184
Elder — 20, 106, 110, 111, 112, 113, 117
Enoch, Order of — 26
Ethics — 190
Evangelism — 28, 97, 98, 125, 140, 151
Evangelist — 107, 114, 126
Excommunication — 130
Executive — 127
Executive Planning Committee — 125
Expulsion — 130

F

Faith — 31, 33, 148, 150, 211
Family Ministry — 124
Far West -- 22, 159
Field Ministries — 115
Field Organization — 124
Financial Law — 171
Financial Services — 122
First Presidency — 29, 107, 115, 126, 172

Forgiveness — 53, 62
Founding — 15
Freedom — 43, 53
Future — 143

G

Gather — 20, 25, 26, 27, 28, 96, 132
Goals — 97
God — 31, 46, 48, 55, 68, 145, 150, 151, 167, 180, 189, 210
Good Sense — 195
Grace — 52, 56
Graceland College — 27, 28, 105
Group — 107, 118, 122, 129
Guide Service — 124
Gurley, Zenas — 25

H

Headquarters — 11, 27
High Priest — 107, 110, 111, 112, 113
History — 12, 15, 125, 179
Holy Spirit — 37, 59, 64, 66, 70, 95, 111, 210
Hope — 14, 144
Human — 41, 48

I

Identity — 185
Illinois — 22
Incarnation — 48
Increase — 170, 172
Independence, MO — 11, 20, 27, 29, 122, 159
Indians — 19

Inheritance — 170
Inspiration — 66, 70, 109
Inspired Version — 72, 78
Interdivisional Council — 126
Invitation — 206

J

Jackson County — 19, 21
Jesus Christ — 37, 47, 60, 68, 86, 87, 91, 92, 98, 114, 143, 145, 150, 151, 180, 210, 214
Joint Council — 126, 129
Judgment — 214
Judicial — 130

K

Kansas City — 116
Kingdom — 13, 14, 54, 93, 141, 146, 150, 158, 212
Kirtland, Ohio — 20, 159

L

Leadership — 124
Legislative — 128
Liberty, Missouri — 22
Lord's Supper — 111, 134
Love — 36, 49, 52, 93, 145, 151, 155, 161, 185, 188, 196

M

Marriage — 112
Membership — 121, 178
Metropolitan Branch — 118
Minister — 28, 104, 124 (See Priesthood)

Mission — 94, 97, 107, 116, 122, 129, 182
Missionary — 18, 26, 107, 127
Missouri — 20
Mormon — 18, 29, 86, 203, (See also Book of Mormon)
Museum — 124
Music — 124

N

Nauvoo, Illinois — 16, 22, 25, 26, 159

O

Objectives — 28, 30, 97
Ohio — 20
Ordain/Ordination — 106, 109, 113, 213
Ordinance — 90, 101, 213
Organization — 17, 115, 182

P

Pastor — 118
Pastoral Care — 96, 124, 136, 184
Pastoral Services — 124
Patriarch — 107, 114, 126
Patriarchal Blessing — 114
Periodicals — 16
Plates — 16
Polygamy — 24, 26, 204
Practice — 132, 183
Prayer — 191
President — 107, 115
Priest — 106, 110, 111, 112, 113
Priesthood — 13, 90, 105, 127, 130, 133, 204

Program Planning — 125
Program Services — 124
Prophet — 18, 24, 30, 88, 129
Protestant — 18
Public Information — 124

R

Reformation — 99
Region — 107, 116, 118, 127, 129, 182
Relationships — 194
Reorganization — 24
Repentance — 46, 62, 152
Response — 46, 62, 101, 185
Restoration — 99
Resurrection — 50, 146, 214
Reunion — 139
Revelation — 18, 25, 35, 55, 70, 213
Rigdon, Sidney — 19, 23
Rules — 193

S

Sacraments — 106, 107, 110, 184
Salvation — 52
Scatter — 96, 140
Scripture — 13, 58, 64, 65, 72, 83, 133, 180, 214
Seventy — 107
Sin — 46, 47
Smith, Frederick — 27, 88, 108
Smith, Hyrum — 23
Smith, Israel — 29, 89, 108
Smith, Joseph, Jr. — 11, 15, 18, 20, 22, 38, 72, 78, 83, 88, 105, 108, 140, 151, 159, 204

Smith, Joseph III — 26, 88, 103, 108
Smith, W. Wallace — 29, 89, 98, 107, 177, 182
Stake — 107, 116, 127, 129, 160, 182
Stewardship — 13, 28, 96, 137, 167, 180, 184, 212
Storehouse — 171
Surplus — 170

T

Teacher — 106
Temple — 20, 105, 160
Theology — 29, 98, 125
Tithing — 13, 138, 172
Trinity — 37

U

Unity — 100

V

Violence — 19, 21

W

Whitmer, Peter, Jr. — 19
Wight, Lyman — 23
Wisconsin — 24
Women — 125, 138
Word (of God) — 59, 70
Word of Wisdom — 196
World — 29, 98, 143, 201, 205
World Conference — 88, 128
Worship — 62, 87, 90, 96, 106, 107, 108, 110, 111, 112, 113, 124, 133, 156, 184

Worth — 54, 98, 136, 154, 180, 196, 198

Y

Young, Brigham — 23
Youth — 138

Z

Zion — 13, 22, 24, 25, 26, 28, 97, 98, 125, 141, 147, 182, 199, 204, 212

AN INTRODUCTION TO THE SAINTS CHURCH

USER'S GUIDE

PREPARED BY PETER A. JUDD

CONTENTS

Introduction to the Book 3
Uses of the Book 5
A Word to the Leader or Teacher Using the Book with Nonmembers 6
Use and Format of the User's Guide 8
CHAPTER 1 SOME HISTORICAL HIGHLIGHTS 10
CHAPTER 2 BELIEVING IN GOD 16
CHAPTER 3 WE'RE ONLY HUMAN 22
CHAPTER 4 JESUS CHRIST 28
CHAPTER 5 REVELATION 34
CHAPTER 6 SCRIPTURE 39
CHAPTER 7 THE BIBLE 44
CHAPTER 8 LATTER DAY SAINT SCRIPTURES 49
CHAPTER 9 THE NATURE AND PURPOSE OF THE CHURCH 55
CHAPTER 10 ALL ARE CALLED 60
CHAPTER 11 CHURCH ORGANIZATION 64
CHAPTER 12 HOW THE CHURCH LIVES 68
CHAPTER 13 WHERE IS THE WORLD GOING? . 73
CHAPTER 14 EVANGELISM 77
CHAPTER 15 ZION 81
CHAPTER 16 STEWARDSHIP 86
CHAPTER 17 WHAT IT MEANS TO BE A MEMBER 91
CHAPTER 18 PERSONAL IDENTITY 95
CHAPTER 19 ETHICS: DECISIONS, DECISIONS, DECISIONS 100
CHAPTER 20 THE SAINTS CHURCH, THE RELIGIOUS COMMUNITY, AND THE WORLD 105

Introduction to the Book

An Introduction to the Saints Church was written as an attempt to acquaint persons with the basic history, belief, organization, and practice of the Saints Church. For those who have grown up in the church or who have spent many years as members much of the content of the book will be familiar. It may serve as a review or a summary for these members. The book may be more helpful for persons who know little or nothing about the church. This will include those who have only recently made contact with the church or who have recently become members. Also included are those who have had no previous contact at all with the church.

This book is unique in many ways. First it represents the viewpoint of its authors at a particular point in time. It is not possible for a descriptive book such as this to "tell it like it is" without bringing in the biases and backgrounds of the persons who wrote it. Had it been written by other persons it would read quite differently. This is why the first word of the title—*An*—is very important. Even though there are not at this time other books in print which cover the same ground as this, it is hoped that someday there will be. Whenever a subject is approached from a number of viewpoints, the reader or viewer has a greater appreciation for what is being studied than if only one source is used.

This book is unique for another reason. Most of the informational materials that have been prepared by members of the Saints Church in the past have been primarily persuasive in their intent. In other words, attractive features have been emphasized, comparisons between the Saints Church and other churches have been included, and the general approach has been that of making the church appear as attractive as possible to potential converts. Such an approach has an important place in the literature of the church. But the intent of *An Introduction to the Saints Church* is different. The authors have attempted to be as objective as possible in their descriptions of the various aspects of the church. They have avoided comparing the claims of the Saints Church with those of other churches.

The presentation is for the most part set in a positive tone, presenting the Saints Church as an organization which is attempting to make a dynamic response to both the call of God and the needs of the world.

To point out all of those things which make the Saints Church different from other churches would be an impossible task. However, the introduction to the book (pages 11-14) does identify five distinguishing elements. The book also describes many beliefs and practices which the Saints Church shares in common with other churches. The concern of the authors in this regard has been to present as complete and balanced a treatment of all aspects of the church as is possible between the covers of a single volume. The bibliography, pages 216-219, lists additional publications to which the reader is referred for deeper discussions of the various subjects introduced in the book.

Uses of the Book

An Introduction to the Saints Church has a number of uses. Individuals who are interested in finding out about the Saints Church may find the book helpful. Members of the church could give or lend copies to their friends or neighbors or purchase copies for public libraries. Congregations and branches could purchase one or more copies for their libraries and additional copies to give to interested nonmembers or to each new member who is baptized.

The book may also be helpful for group study. Church school classes (youth or adults), special classes for new members, or group meetings in homes for interested nonmembers are just a few uses that this book may have in groups.

The book can be used as the basis for study in greater depth by individuals or groups. Upon completion of this book students can use one or more of the books listed in the bibliography on pages 216-219 of the book or other books of their own choosing.

A Word to the Leader or Teacher Using the Book with Nonmembers

Members may wish to use *An Introduction to the Saints Church* as an aid in interesting nonmembers in the church. It would seem appropriate to say here that membership in the Saints Church involves both an understanding of history, belief, organization and practice and a commitment to the living Christ.

This book provides some information which will assist the nonmember in gaining familiarity with various aspects of the Saints Church. Such familiarity is important. However, even an in-depth understanding of how the church operates, its history, belief, and practice does not of itself make one a disciple. Discipleship is more a matter of following a person (Christ) than it is adherence to a set of beliefs. In fact, overemphasis on correctness of doctrine can lead to idolatry.

It is imperative for member and potential member alike to supplement their understanding of matters covered in the book with a vital relationship with and commitment to Christ. To receive the gospel is to receive the Christ because he is, in the fullest sense, the gospel.

There are those who are seeking answers to basic questions about life. It is proper to think that what the church has to offer will answer some of these. But the church can never answer all questions or prescribe an unambiguous code of behavior. Following Christ and holding membership in the church are matters of faith. Faith requires us to make our own decisions guided by the Holy Spirit and to trust that the future is in God's hands even though we don't know all the answers.

The importance of the leader or teacher cannot be overemphasized. Leaders must resist the temptation to try to give their own testimonies and belief systems to others. The spirit in which the leader approaches other persons should be that of inviting them to acquire a personal testimony of Christ. It is neither advisable nor in the final analysis possible to give our faith to others. They have to find their own faith. Leaders are responsible for assisting them in this process.

USE AND FORMAT OF THE USER'S GUIDE

This *User's Guide* can be of help to

a) an individual reading the book alone
b) a leader or teacher working with a group studying the book, and/or
c) participants in a group studying the book

The book itself is divided into twenty chapters varying in length from five to twelve pages. In addition, there is a preface, introduction, invitation, and appendix. The *User's Guide* is organized along the same lines. For each chapter of the book, the *User's Guide* includes the following:

1. *Introduction.* An introduction to the subject of the chapter.

2. *Chapter Overview.* A one- or two-sentence summary for each of the major subsections of the chapter.

3. *Important Concepts.* Several important concepts that the author intends the reader to become acquainted with.

4. *Questions for Response.* Questions to which the reader is invited to respond. Space is provided for written responses to each question in the *User's Guide.* The majority of these questions are appropriate for persons with little or no familiarity with the Saints Church as well as for persons with some background. These questions can be responded to by individuals or discussed in a group.

5. *Activities and Research.* Suggestions appropriate for persons studying the book in groups. Some suggestions invite persons to do individual reading in books listed in the bibliography and other sources. Many of these outside reading suggestions can also be followed by individuals studying the book on their own.

6. *Conclusion.* A short paragraph which focuses on the central thrust of the chapter and how persons can relate it to their lives.

Individuals and groups using the book and *User's Guide* will have widely varying backgrounds with respect to the Saints Church. Leaders working with groups will want to choose carefully from the questions and activity suggestions in the *User's Guide.* These leaders will need to keep in mind how familiar group members are with the history, belief, organization, and practices of the Saints Church. Some questions and activity suggestions that are appropriate for use with a group of established members may be entirely inappropriate for nonmembers. The reverse may also be true.

CHAPTER 1

SOME HISTORICAL HIGHLIGHTS

Introduction

This chapter describes selected events from the history of the Saints Church. It is obviously impossible to include anything like a complete history in the space of one short chapter. The "official" history of the church now extends to eight volumes and still does not describe the events of the last thirty years. In spite of the impossibility of trying to recount the history of the church in one chapter, these historical highlights are presented so that the reader will be familiar with the historical framework surrounding the matters of church doctrine, organization, and practice explained in subsequent chapters.

Chapter Overview

1. *Joseph Smith's initial claims.* In this section, Joseph Smith's experiences leading up to the publication of the Book of Mormon and the official organization of the church (March and April, 1830, respectively) are highlighted. The Saints are depicted as a "peculiar" people frequently experiencing persecution at the hands of their neighbors.

2. *The early church, 1830-1847.* The Saints engaged in many struggles as they attempted to live according to their understanding of God's will for them. They migrated

westward, spending time at Kirtland, Ohio; Independence and Far West, Missouri; and Nauvoo, Illinois, where Joseph and Hyrum Smith were martyred in 1844.

3. *Dispersion of the church.* Following the death of its founder, the church splintered into a number of groups.

4. *The Reorganization.* The Reorganized Church began under the leadership of Jason Briggs and Zenas H. Gurley, Sr.

5. *1860-1914.* These years cover the presidency of Joseph Smith III, son of the founder.

6. *1914-1946.* These are the years of the presidency of the founder's grandson, Frederick M. Smith.

7. *Since 1946.* Some of the important trends of the last thirty years are discussed in this section.

Important Concepts

1. The Saints Church had its beginning at a time of intense religious excitement in frontier America.

2. The charismatic personality and creativity of Joseph Smith were in large part responsible for the growth of the Saints in the early years.

3. The Book of Mormon was the primary missionary tool of the infant church.

4. The church was highly mobile, geographically.

5. The church was, in its early years, the subject of intense, sometimes violent, persecution, a major factor in its mobility.

6. The establishment of God's kingdom on earth (Zion) was sensed as an urgent calling and responsibility.

7. Prior to Joseph Smith's death in 1844 the church became more and more interested in otherworldly concerns and less interested in the here and now.

8. The Saints Church has in recent years responded in new ways to the call to be God's agent of ministry to his

world in need, especially as it has confronted the implications of work in non-Western cultures.

Questions for Response

1. How do you react, personally, to the claims of Joseph Smith(pages15-17)? Try to understand how the people of his time both inside and outside the church might have responded. What particular responses and observations can you make about each claim?

____

____

____

2. On pages 19-23 the Saints are depicted as a people constantly on the move (New York, Ohio, Missouri, Illinois). What are some reasons for this high degree of mobility?

____

____

____

3. What might have been some reasons for the death of Joseph Smith? What effects did it have on the church?

____

____

4. What appear to have been some of the factors giving rise to the Reorganization? Why do you suppose these people did not go west with the majority or give more permanent allegiance to some of the other factional leaders with whom some of them associated briefly in the 1840s and 1850s?

5. What were the main characteristics of the church during the presidency of Joseph Smith III? What were some of his major contributions to the church?

6. What were the main characteristics of the church and the major contributions of President Frederick M. Smith during the period 1914-1946?

7. What have been the main characteristics of the church and the major contributions of its presidents since 1946?

Activities and Research

1. Suggest that some participants role play Joseph Smith telling of some of his early experiences while others role play persons who are hearing him. Other persons could play the parts of early church missionaries who told persons about the Book of Mormon. Talk about how you felt playing the various parts.

2. Have persons research *The History of the Reorganized Church of Jesus Christ of Latter Day Saints,* Volumes 1-8, to find out more about some of the events recounted in this chapter, or other events of interest not covered in it. Use the indexes at the back of the Church History volumes to locate the information. Ask these persons to make brief reports and be prepared to answer questions on the subjects they have researched.

3. Try to find someone who has done some reading in the area of early nineteenth-century American history, preferably religious history. Ask that person to meet with the group and give a short presentation on the social setting of the period. An excellent source for this information is found in two Herald House books by Wayne Ham—*Publish Glad Tidings* (1970, pages 17-25) and *Yesterday's Horizons* (1975, pages 134-138). See also *The Burned-Over District* by Whitney R. Cross (Harper Torchbook) and Winthrop Hudson's splendid survey, *Religion in America* (Charles Scribner's Sons, 1965). An understanding of the period and

culture in which the church took root will help one to understand both the positive and the negative reactions that it provoked.

4. Suggest that someone do some reading in Roy Cheville's *Scriptures from Ancient America* (especially chapters 4-6, 10, and 30) to provide some general information on the development of the Book of Mormon and its message. A brief report would be in order here. The subject can be treated in greater depth in your study of Chapter 8.

5. Robert Flanders' *Nauvoo: Kingdom on the Mississippi* (University of Illinois Press, 1965) is probably the best book available on the Saints in Illinois, 1839-1946. An oral review of this book would provide many insights into the spectacular growth and eclipse of the church at Nauvoo.

6. Invite an alert older member to tell the group of the changes that have occurred in the church during the last fifty years. Let members of the group quiz the visitor. Which changes appear to be improvements? Which changes have had a negative impact? Which ones have had both positive and negative influences in the life of the church?

Conclusion

An understanding of the Saints' past rewards one with insights into who they are today and what they are about. The Saints have made bold claims and in so doing have alienated many. They have sensed a call to be God's people. Sometimes they have succeeded; at other times they have failed. They are proud of much of their history; it tells the story of their struggles and it gives them a unique identity.

CHAPTER 2

BELIEVING IN GOD

Introduction

All religions profess belief in a form, existence, or reality that is in some sense above, beyond, or more basic than humanity. We call this God. Christians and Jews look to the God testified to in Old Testament writings as their God, the creator and sustainer of all that is. As a Christian denomination, the Saints believe in this God. They hold this belief in common with other Christians and Jews. Integral to a belief in God is the affirmation that God cannot be completely understood, explained, or experienced by humanity. Therefore this chapter deals not with a description of God as a definable reality but rather with the process of believing in God. This believing is a process of responding to and articulating in part a reality that we cannot completely comprehend.

Chapter Overview

The following are the main points covered in this chapter:

1. *God is always greater than our knowledge of him.* Relating to God is always a matter of faith in that God defies description and full comprehension. It is possible to say something about God. But we must always keep in

mind that our understandings are less than complete.

2. *God is personal.* God expresses characteristics that we have come to associate with personhood, e.g. love.

3. *God acts in history and reveals himself.* Here God is affirmed as having purpose, as being active rather than passive. God reveals himself in the stream of human history.

4. *God is the creator and sustainer of the universe.* All that exists does so by the power of God's creative nature. God continues to be interested in what he has created; he sustains the world.

5. *God is love.* The supreme expression of God is his love for those he has created. This love is expressed most fully in the person of Jesus Christ, God's son.

6. *God is one.* The concept of the trinity refers to the three expressions of God which nevertheless represent a unity in purpose and character.

7. *The nature of belief and doctrine.* Written or spoken statements of belief or doctrine have limitations. We can never completely describe God in words; neither can we communicate personal experiences to others without error.

Important Concepts

1. God is beyond our complete comprehension. Therefore anything we say or write about God is less than an exact description of reality.

2. We affirm the existence of God as a result of experiences we have had in which we have felt God's presence in our lives.

3. We are able to describe God as creator and sustainer, as personal, as love, etc., based on our experiences.

4. Belief in God is a matter of faith. It cannot be proven. Those who have faith in God live *as if* the existence of deity were a proven fact even though it is not.

Questions for Response

1. What are some experiences in your life when you have felt the presence of God or in some other way felt sure that God exists?

___

___

___

2. List some attributes of God. Which of these have you experienced in relationship with God? Which have you read about (for instance in the Bible)? Do all of these characteristics seem consistent with each other?

___

___

___

3. In what different ways can God be considered *personal?* The book describes some; can you think of others?

___

___

___

4. This chapter describes God as revealing himself. What particular expressions of God's self-revelation have *you* experienced?

5. What different kinds of things can you think of that God created? Are there things that you feel God did not create?

6. Why is love considered as the basic or central characteristic of God? Where do you see God's love being expressed today?

7. Think for a moment about the difficult concept of the trinity. Try to write your own one-sentence definition of each of the three expressions of God (Father, Son, and Holy Spirit).

8. What can you do to better understand God?

9. What can you do to exercise greater faith in God?

Activities and Research

1. Ask one or two members of the class to read pages 16-29 and 52-61 of *Exploring the Faith* (Herald House, 1970). Then ask these persons to facilitate a group discussion on one or more aspects of God.

2. As a group try to write a short, clear statement of belief

in God. You may wish to start out by having each group member write an individual statement and then combine them into one. When you have finished, compare the statement with paragraph one on page 210 of the book. What similarities and differences are notable?

3. Do some research in Scripture. Using concordances to the Three Standard Books, look up references to God or to a specific attribute of God such as "love of God," "power of God," "will of God," or "grace of God." Allow time for the researchers to make short reports on their findings to the class.

4. An important part of responding to God's self-revelation is being willing to follow where God leads even though we don't know completely where we will end up. This requires faith—faith that God knows what he is doing. As a group, what is one specific way that you can respond to the leadings of the Holy Spirit by doing something that you feel called to do but are hesitant to start because uncertainty exists? Make plans to move out in faith, starting today.

Conclusion

God is very real in the lives of human beings even though we don't know everything about him. This requires us to exercise faith and recognize the limitations of our own understandings and interpretations. God's supreme characteristic is love for all creation. This love is evidenced most powerfully in Jesus Christ. The reality we call God elicits a response of allegiance that as persons we might live in harmony with each other according to God's purposes for us.

CHAPTER 3

WE'RE ONLY HUMAN

Introduction

As human beings we live in a world composed of other human beings, other animals, vegetable and mineral forms. These basic forms and the intricate institutions that we have created make up the social context in which we live. Each of us has a wide range of experiences each day of our lives. We react to our experiences in varying ways. We feel good about some, bad about others, and there are even some to which we are indifferent. Whatever our individual circumstances, we live in a complex world which provides both happiness and frustration. We attempt to make sense out of our world and see some purpose to our lives.

Chapter Overview

The following are the main points covered in this chapter.

1. *Living in between.* Our existence is described as being between extremes. We are between life and death, between good and evil, between freedom and restriction, between aloneness and community, and between joy and sorrow. Our lives are mixtures of many experiences.

2. *Separation and togetherness.* Our existence between

extremes sometimes causes us to become separated from ourselves, others, and God. At other times, however, we experience a sense of wholeness, unity, or togetherness in these relationships.

3. *Living in bondage.* Separation leads to bondage—that is, lack of freedom. We experience bondage to the past (guilt), to the present (meaninglessness), and to the future (despair).

4. *Responding to our situation.* We are free to respond to those situations in which we find ourselves. When we rebel against God we find ourselves estranged from him (sin). The appropriate response to this condition is confession and an acceptance of redemption which God offers to us.

Important Concepts

1. All persons experience a wide variety of things to which they react in various ways.

2. Feelings of anger, fear, hostility, mistrust, etc., are a normal part of the everyday experience of persons. "Bad" feelings are not to be suppressed or something to feel guilty about. Rather we must learn to express them in responsible ways.

3. Making decisions, as frustrating, time consuming, and emotionally tiring as this process often is, represents an important part of what it means to be a person.

4. Separation and bondage are characteristic parts of the lives of all of us. We can never completely get rid of them, but we can reduce their frequency and not allow them to dominate our lives.

5. Most importantly, we do not live life alone. God is with us and cares about us. He has endowed our lives with meaning and has provided the avenue for our salvation from sin. We are invited to respond to his grace.

Questions for Response

1. Illustrate from your own life experiences how you live "in between." What decisions can you make that will move you from an undesirable extreme to a desirable one?

____

____

____

____

2. Is freedom desirable? List some of the advantages and some of the disadvantages of gaining greater freedom. How are you defining freedom?

____

____

____

3. Give one example of how you have experienced or are experiencing separation from God. Also give an example of your separation from yourself and one example of your separation from another person. In each case, what can you do to move from separation to togetherness?

____

____

____

4. Give one example each of your own feelings of guilt (bondage to past), meaninglessness (bondage to present), and despair (bondage to future). How can you move from bondage to responsible freedom in each case?

___

___

___

5. What are some evidences of sin in your life? What can you do to repent from these?

___

___

___

Activities and Research

1. Ask one person to read pages 90-102 of *Exploring the Faith* (Herald House, 1970). This person could then facilitate a group discussion centering on the human experience.

2. As a group try to write a short, clear statement of belief about humanity. You may wish to start out by having each member write an individual statement and then combining these into one. When you have finished, compare your finished statement with paragraph six on page 211 of the book. What similarities and differences are notable?

3. As individuals, make charts diagramming the various relationships that you experience during a typical day. The

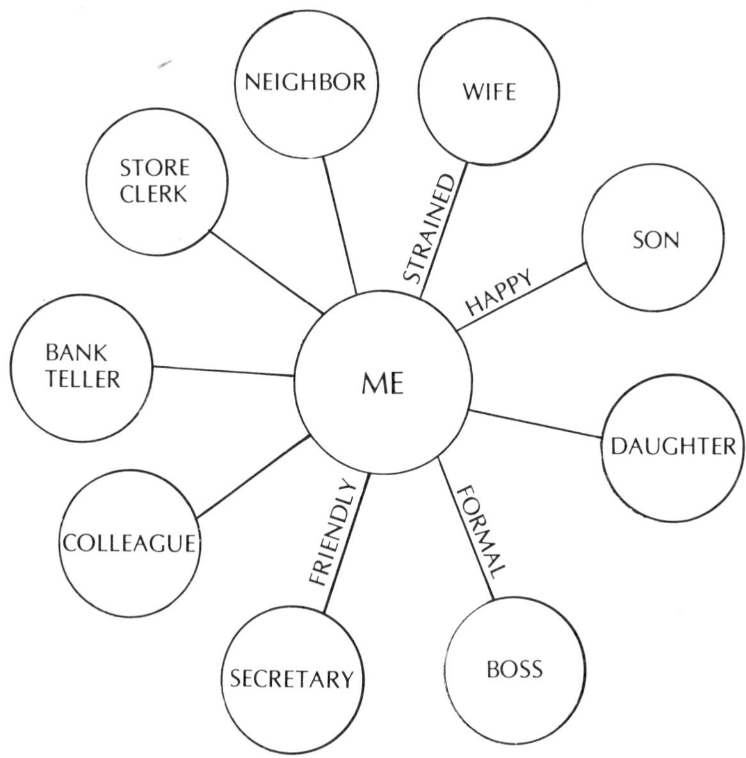

diagram shows one way that this could be done. Describe each relationship in a word characterizing your experience with that person on a given day. You may wish to use words such as "happy," "strained," "formal," "friendly," etc. Share your diagrams with others in the group. What do the diagrams tell about the group members?

4. Suggest that group members volunteer to tell of an experience and/or relationship in their lives for the group to talk about. Have other members had similar experiences? How might the relationship be improved?

Conclusion

We all live our lives in relationship with other people. Sometimes we experience fulfillment, significance, happiness. At other times we experience frustration, meaninglessness, self-pity. True community exists only where individuals recognize each other's uniqueness and offer themselves in mutual support of each other. Each of us has unrealized potential which can only be realized as we respond in greater measure to God's love for us. By the power of God, lives dominated by fear can come to fruition and joy.

CHAPTER 4

JESUS CHRIST

Introduction

Jesus Christ is at the very center of the Christian faith. When asked what were the fundamental principles of the religion of the Saints, Joseph Smith once said, "The fundamental principle of our religion is the testimony of the apostles and prophets concerning Jesus Christ, 'that he died, was buried, and rose again the third day, and ascended into heaven'; and all other things are only appendages to these, which pertain to our religion."* Each of the Three Standard Books of the church confirms this. It is through Jesus Christ that God expresses love for all humanity and grants salvation to us; we cannot save ourselves. Without Jesus Christ we as individuals and as a church would not have any basis for hope or for a meaningful present.

Chapter Overview

The following are the main points covered in this chapter:

1. *The ministry of Jesus Christ.* Jesus Christ is God in human form. He expressed in his life on earth a rare

---

**Elder's Journal*, Vol. I, No. 3 (July 1838), page 44.

compassion for and acceptance of people. He demonstrated the characteristics that Christians generally attribute to God. Jesus was fully divine and fully human at the same time.

2. *The Crucifixion.* By being willing to die, Jesus Christ shows God's deep concern for humanity. The crucifixion also shows the intensity of human sin and our rejection of all that Jesus stood for.

3. *The Resurrection.* In this central event God shows that death cannot be victorious. God won victory over death and hate and reaffirmed those principles for which Jesus Christ stood. The resurrection testifies to the eternal nature of life.

4. *Salvation through Jesus Christ.* Human beings are unable to save themselves from guilt, meaninglessness, and despair. Through Jesus Christ, God gives us salvation freely. We cannot deserve it; it is a free gift.

5. *New possibilities in Christ.* The salvation given us in Jesus Christ endows our lives with new possibilities. We are released from bondage to new freedom.

Important Concepts

1. Jesus Christ is central to the faith. Nothing else is more important. All other beliefs are of secondary importance when compared to God's self-revelation in Christ.

2. Jesus' life was his message. He lived the kind of life God wants us all to live. His spoken message and his actions supported each other.

3. Jesus' death was an extension of his life. They both express the principle of giving of self for others.

4. Jesus' resurrection establishes right as victor over wrong.

5. Jesus' life, death, and resurrection illustrated God's unending love for all creation.

6. Salvation in Christ is not conditional on our good works. We cannot deserve it. God loves us in spite of anything that we have done or will do.

7. We can become new persons in Christ. By accepting and responding to God's love, we are changed.

Questions for Response

1. The affirmation that Jesus Christ is both fully human and fully divine defies rational explanation. Think about it for a while. What does it mean to you? have you tended to emphasize more the divine or the human nature of Jesus?

____

____

____

2. What do you see in the life of Jesus which brings you to a greater realization of what it means to be human?

____

____

____

3. Examine the scripture from Luke 4:18-19 on page 49. How did Jesus "preach good news to the poor"? How did he "proclaim release to the captives"? How did he proclaim recovering of sight to the blind"? How did he "set at liberty

those who are oppressed"? How did he "proclaim the acceptable year of the Lord"? How can you do each of these things?

4. How was Jesus "the man for others"?

5. What does Christ's crucifixion mean *to you*?

6. What does Christ's resurrection mean *to you*?

7. A popular question in some religious circles is, "Have you been saved?" After reading this chapter how would you respond to this question? Explain your answer.

8. Specifically, what new possibilities are available to you in Jesus Christ?

Activities and Research

1. Ask one member of the group to read pages 30-51 of *Exploring the Faith* (Herald House, 1970). This person could then facilitate a discussion on the significance of Jesus Christ to the church.

2. Suggest that the group try to develop a short statement

of belief concerning Jesus Christ. When this has been done compare the statement with paragraph two on page 208 What are the similarities and differences?

3. Ask one or two persons to research the Doctrine and Covenants and/or Book of Mormon to find indications of the importance of Christ to the people concerned. Provide time for these individuals to make reports to the class.

4. Jesus Christ was the foundation of the New Testament Church. Ask one or more persons to research the book of Acts and the New Testament letters of Paul and others for evidence of this. Use a Bible Concordance and, if available, a Bible Commentary. Allow time for reports to the group.

5. Arrange for a sharing or testimony time for persons to talk about their experiences with the ever living Christ. How has Christ changed their lives?

6. As a group, carefully analyze the scripture from Philippians found on page 47. What does it say to *you?* Talk about parts that are difficult to understand.

Conclusion

Jesus Christ is more than a person who lived almost two thousand years ago. He is alive and present in the world today. He is our Savior without whom our lives would be without meaning. Christ is the center and foundation of the church. He continually calls us to repentance and to acceptance of God's unconditional love for us.

CHAPTER 5

REVELATION

Introduction

The Saints have always stressed the reality of God's revelation. They affirm that God reveals himself to persons in all ages. It is his nature to reveal himself so that we as human beings can gain some appreciation of God's nature and his purposes for us. God also invites us to respond to his self-disclosure.

Chapter Overview

The following are the main points covered in this chapter:

1. *WHAT and WHY does God reveal?* God does not reveal ideas or propositions *about* himself but he reveals *himself*. It is God's nature to do this so that his creation can experience him.

2. *HOW and TO WHOM does God reveal himself?* God makes himself known by acting in the affairs of persons. God is also revealed in the things and beings that he has created. God does not reveal himself to only a select few at certain points in time but to all persons in all ages.

3. *God reveals himself in Jesus Christ.* Jesus Christ is the central revelation of God. He is both the medium and the message of God's revelation.

4. *The RESPONSE to revelation.* God's revelation invites response. When perceiving this revelation we attempt to share our experiences with others. We make spoken and written responses and interpretations. We may also decide to pursue a course of action prompted by the revelation we perceive.

Important Concepts

1. God reveals himself to persons of all ages and places. He is no respecter of persons.
2. God reveals himself by his action among people and by his creative and sustaining power.
3. The term *Word of God* refers to God's actions and deeds.
4. Jesus Christ is the most important and basic expression of God's revelation. In Christ God reveals himself in a manner most suitable to human comprehension.
5. God's revelation invites persons to *respond.* It demands that we act to change our lives, making them more expressive of our God-given potential.

Questions for Response

1. Why has a belief in revelation been so important to the Saints through the years? Is it important to you? Why or why not?

____

____

____

2. Consider why God reveals himself. A couple of reasons are found on pages 56 and 57. Can you think of others? Which reasons are more appealing to you?

____

____

____

3. How and when have you experienced God's revelation in your life? What experiences of God's revelation have you heard other people tell about?

____

____

____

4. What characteristics of God are evident as a result of his revelation to persons? To you?

____

____

____

5. The book suggests that Jesus Christ is the most important revelation of God. What makes him so central?

____

6. What characteristics of God are revealed in Jesus Christ?

7. How have you responded to God's revelation? What did you write or tell others? What action did you take?

Activities and Research

1. Ask group members to look up references to some of God's "mighty acts" in the Old Testament (see for example Exodus 14 and Ezra 1, 2). What did the people seem to be feeling as these events were occurring? In the group discuss the biblical accounts.

2. Ask a class member to look up references in the four gospels which illustrate Jesus acknowledging dependence on God or being sent by God. Suggest that the group talk about how these incidents are examples of Jesus being the central expression of God.

3. Invite each member to choose a partner and then have persons share information about themselves with their partners. What has each partner learned? What did they learn about their partners which was not spoken? In what different ways did persons reveal themselves? As a total group talk about how the self-revealing experience in pairs was similar to and different from God's revelation to persons.

4. Ask for volunteers who are willing to share an experience with the group. Preferably it should be an account of an experience when the persons have felt the presence of God in their lives but it could be an experience of an encounter with another person. How easy was it for the persons to describe their experiences? How easy was it for listeners to understand? What did the persons *do* as a response to the experiences?

5. True worship is usually accompanied by a profound awareness of the presence of God. Invite persons to tell of worship experiences in which they have encountered God. What made these experiences special? Perhaps the group would like to plan a short worship service for your next meeting centering on the theme "God makes himself known." Follow the worship experience with a few minutes of evaluation and reflection.

Conclusion

God is continually making himself known to persons. Too often we are not receptive to this revelation. God reveals himself in numerous ways according to his wisdom and our needs. If we are to be disciples of Christ we must open all our senses to more significant and frequent experience with God. In so doing, we can become more like the persons we were intended to be—living in harmony with each other in God's image.

CHAPTER 6

SCRIPTURE

Introduction

Scripture is a vital element in the life of the Saints Church. It represents accumulated testimony of those who have experienced God at work in the lives of people. It also preserves a record of persons who have struggled to live up to the demands they perceived God to be making on them. Scripture is an important resource to the contemporary church as a body and to its members as individuals.

Chapter Overview

The following are the main points covered in this chapter:

1. *What is Scripture?* Scripture is a compilation of selected written interpretations of God's revelatory acts and of human responses to these acts.

2. *How writings become Scripture.* Those writings which are considered by the church to have enduring value to its life are recognized as Scripture by being canonized.

3. *The role of Scripture.* Scripture is authoritative because it speaks to the situations and needs of people and because it has a long tradition of acceptance in the church. Scripture speaks to specific situations (timely) but is also of enduring value (timeless).

4. *Scholarship and interpretation.* All persons who read

or hear Scripture are involved in the process of interpretation. We ask what the meaning of Scripture is for us today.

5. *Open Scripture.* Scripture is open to new insights and interpretations. It is also open in the sense that new scripture can be added to the canon.

Important Concepts

1. Scripture contains words written by human beings. However, we affirm that the scripture writers were *inspired* by the Holy Spirit in their attempts to faithfully interpret their experiences.

2. Scripture provides us with insights into the people and events of the past and how those people dealt with the important challenges of life.

3. Scripture is useful and authoritative for us as it helps us deal with the questions we face in daily life.

4. The words of Scripture are subject to human interpretation. We each bring our unique backgrounds to Scripture study and come away with different understandings.

5. If we are to use Scripture responsibly we must let it speak to us rather than approach it with our minds made up.

Questions for Response

1. What is your understanding of Scripture? Write out your own single sentence definition of "Scripture."

---

2. It could be said that Scripture is the result of God and persons working together. What do you see as God's contribution? What do you see as the human contribution?

3. What do you understand to be the nature of inspiration? Have you ever felt inspired? Describe the experience.

4. What value does Scripture have in *your* life? Which passages of Scripture are particularly meaningful to you? Why?

5. How would you go about studying Scripture? How important do you think scriptural scholarship is? Explain your answer.

6. What are some ways that you can consider Scripture as open to new interpretations? Read one or two familiar passages of Scripture carefully. What new understandings emerge?

Activities and Research

1. Do some research on the concept of canonization. How did the Bible become what it is today? Invite group members to talk about this process.

2. Suggest that group members share passages of Scripture that are particularly meaningful for them. Why are they meaningful? What different understandings do other members of the group have of these scriptures?

3. What *authority* do group members see Scripture having? Talk about authority in the context of the discussion on pages 67-68. Do persons see scriptural authority as primarily external or internal?

4. Ask several persons to research the situations to which selected scriptures were addressed. Ask them to make reports to the group emphasizing the "timely" aspects of the scriptures. Then ask other persons to suggest how these same scriptures are "timeless" in the way that they relate to today.

5. Invite one person to read Exploration Sixteen (pages 109-112) of *The Burning Bush* by Geoffrey Spencer (Herald House, 1975). This exploration talks about scriptural scholarship. Schedule time for discussion of this subject. Some members of the class may wish to pursue critical study of selected passages of Scripture.

Conclusion

Scripture testifies to God at work in the world. It also illustrates human struggles to achieve a level of existence in harmony with God's purposes. We can learn much from Scripture if we let it speak to our lives. It does not provide us with precise answers to life's dilemmas but offers guidance for making our own decisions. Scripture is one of the richest resources that Christians have today.

CHAPTER 7

THE BIBLE

Introduction

Recognition of the Bible as Scripture is one of the most important elements that the Saints Church has in common with other Christian denominations. The Bible is a fascinating compilation of written documents representing a wide variety of literary styles. It has stood the test of time as a valuable resource to Christians individually and within church groups.

Chapter Overview

The following are the main points covered in this chapter:

1. *What is the Bible?* The Bible is a collection of books written at various times, in various circumstances, by various people. It has gone through a long, complex process of editing and translating which is still not complete today.

2. *The Old Testament.* This is the first of two sections of the Bible containing materials relating to the pre-Christian era. It can be subdivided into the following sections: books of law, books of history, books of poetry, and the major and minor prophets.

3. *The New Testament.* This is the second section containing materials relating to the Christian Era. It can be

subdivided into the following sections: the Gospels and Acts, the letters of Paul, and other writings.

4. *The Inspired Version.* This is a new translation published from manuscripts prepared by Joseph Smith, Jr.

5. *Using the Bible today.* Even though it is many hundreds and thousands of years old, the Bible is the best-selling book of all time. It is used by millions of persons today.

Important Concepts

1. The Bible is not a single book telling a continuous story but rather constitutes a collection of many separately authored books.

2. The books of the Bible were not written for intended inclusion in a canon of sacred writing. Instead, they went through many years of use before being accepted as authoritative by the Christian church.

3. The Inspired Version is unique to the Saints' Church. It represents Joseph Smith's attempt to clarify ambiguities, correct what he thought to be errors, and in other ways make the Bible more meaningfully represent the word of God.

4. The Bible is most useful when we approach it with an open mind, letting it speak to us in our present-day situations.

Questions for Response

1. Which of the *books* of the Bible are you most familiar with? Can you give reasons?

____

____

2. Which of the many *versions* of the Bible available today are you familiar with? What are some of the advantages and disadvantages of the various versions? Which is your favorite version?

3. What are some of the differences between the Inspired and King James versions of which you are aware? Which are, in your mind, important? What are some examples of verses where the Inspired Version makes the meaning clearer for you?

4. What can you do to make the Bible speak more effectively to your life today? Be specific.

5. Describe a plan of Bible study that would most effectively enrich your life.

Activities and Research

1. Ask someone to obtain a copy of the Apocrypha and briefly review its contents for the benefit of the group. Are there books that seem like they should have been included in the Bible? If so, give reasons. An alternate procedure if enough copies of the Apocrypha are available is to have each member review one or two books (there are fourteen in all) and make a case for their inclusion in the canon.

2. Obtain as many different versions of the Bible as you can. Look up several verses and as a group discuss which versions give the most understandable renditions. One verse to use might be Romans 3:20.

3. Ask each group member to read one of the minor prophets (the last twelve books of the Old Testament). Then provide opportunity for reports and discussion on the messages of the prophets chosen. How are they different? How similar?

4. Ask each person to read one of the general epistles in the New Testament (James, Jude, I or II Peter, or I, II, or III John). Follow the procedure described in Activity 3 above.

5. Obtain a copy of *Joseph Smith's "New Translation" of the Bible* (Herald House, 1970) and read the three introductory articles by F. Henry Edwards (pages 7-24). These same articles are found in the November 15, December 1, and December 15, 1967, issues of the *Saints'*

Herald. They deal with the Inspired Version. Ask whoever does this reading to make a presentation and facilitate a discussion on the significance of the Inspired Version. Another source to consult on this subject if the above mentioned are not available is Exploration Six (pages 50-54) in *The Burning Bush* by Geoffrey Spencer (Herald House, 1975).

Conclusion

The Bible has been called the "Book of Ages." It is a powerful testimony of the actions of God in the lives of persons. It is a valuable tool for those who are seeking the most effective way to be disciples of Christ in these challenging times.

CHAPTER 8

LATTER DAY SAINT SCRIPTURES

In addition to the Bible, the Saints Church has two other books of Scripture: the Book of Mormon and Doctrine and Covenants. These together with the Bible are known as the "Three Standard Books" of the church. This chapter introduces these other two books, giving information about their origin, content, and use.

Chapter Overview

The following are the main points covered in this chapter:

1. *What is the Book of Mormon and where did it come from?* The Book of Mormon was presented to the church as a record of ancient inhabitants of America. Joseph Smith dictated the book to scribes who prepared the manuscript from which it was published in 1830.

2. *What story does the Book of Mormon tell?* The Book of Mormon consists of a number of separate books named after different individuals. The story begins with the migration of a colony of people from Jerusalem to the new world around 600 B.C. and concludes with their destruction around A.D. 400.

3. *How is the Book of Mormon used today?* It is used by individuals and groups within the Saints Church as inspirational literature similar to the way Christians use the Bible.

4. *What is the Doctrine and Covenants and what does it contain?* This is a compilation of documents that the church accepts as representing "the mind and will of God." The various sections are, for the most part, authored by the prophet (president) of the church and offer instruction and counsel directed toward persons and situations.

5. *Using the Doctrine and Covenants today.* It is used as a source of inspirational literature as are the other two standard books. It is also used as a standard of law for the Saints Church.

Important Concepts

1. From the time of its initial appearance to the present day, the Book of Mormon has been the subject of much speculation, attack, and subsequent defense.

2. Very little is known abut the precise way in which Joseph Smith produced the book. His testimony was simply that it was done "by the gift and power of God."

3. Members of the church past and present have differing views as to the role that the Book of Mormon plays in their own lives and the role they think it should play in the church.

4. The Book of Mormon and Doctrine and Covenants are designed to be used *in addition to* and not *instead of* the Bible. They each testify to a living God who makes himself known in his Son Jesus Christ.

5. The Doctrine and Covenants is a collection of timely documents addressed to various specific situations. Its present-day use is best governed by this reality.

6. Like the Bible, these other two books of Scripture can speak to us today if we remain open to new understandings that can come from prayerful study.

Questions for Response

1. What is your initial reaction to the idea that books other than the Bible can be considered as Scripture? What is it about your own past that conditions this reaction?

____

____

____

____

2. If other books are to be considered Scripture, what criteria would you like to see them live up to?

____

____

____

____

3. Does the Book of Mormon sound like something you would be interested in reading? Why or why not? If you have already read it try to imagine that you have not.

____

____

____

____

4. Which of the four views of the Book of Mormon listed on page 87 appeals to you most? Why?

---

5. Does the Doctrine and Covenants sound like something you would be interested in reading? Why or why not? If you have already read it try to imagine that you have not.

---

6. What do you think are the most important uses of a book like the Doctrine and Covenants?

Activities and Research

1. Suggest that one or more members of the group do research into the coming forth of the Book of Mormon. Sources are Church History, Volume 1; *Scriptures from Ancient America* by Roy Cheville, Chapter 6; and *The Burning Bush* by Geoffrey Spencer, Exploration Eight. The researchers can then make oral reports and facilitate a discussion on the subject.

2. Using Cheville's *Scriptures from Ancient America* and the outline found on pages 85 and 86 of the book, develop a more detailed summary of the content of the Book of Mormon. For each of the items on the outline you could write one to three paragraphs. This would be a project for a number of persons. The completed overview of the Book of Mormon could be typed up and photocopied so that each member of the group could have a copy.

3. Refer to the four views of the Book of Mormon on page 87. Ask four participants, one for each view, to be responsible for developing a case supporting the views. Schedule time for oral presentation and discussions. Remember that any person can subscribe to all of the views without contradiction. Are there other views that are important to persons in your group?

4. Ask each class member to choose one section from the Doctrine and Covenants. Allow time for individual research into the background behind each section. An excellent source for this information is F. Henry Edwards' *Commentary on the Doctrine and Covenants* which is now out of print. Try to borrow one or more copies of this book from church members who have them. Another source would be the eight volumes of Church History. Suggest that reports be given and discussion center on the *timely* and *timeless* aspects of each document.

5. Which passages of the Book of Mormon or Doctrine and Covenants are the favorites of group members? Invite persons to give reasons for the passages they have selected.

6. Ask the group to discuss how the two distinctive Scriptures of the Saints Church might be used more effectively by individuals within the church and by the church as a corporate body.

Conclusion

The Saints are blessed with unique resources in the Book of Mormon and Doctrine and Covenants. They are challenged to make full use of these by allowing the Scriptures to speak to their lives today. The Scriptures are an effective tool to change the lives of people. Used under the guidance of God's Holy Spirit they can significantly increase the contributions of the Saints toward God's work in his world today.

CHAPTER 9

THE NATURE AND PURPOSE OF THE CHURCH

Introduction

The church means many things to many people. Among other views, however, it is important that the church be seen as a *community of people* identified by a common calling and allegiance. The church exists in the world, called by God to assist in his work of redemption.

Chapter Overview

The following are the main points covered in this chapter:

1. *Calling and purpose.* The church is the "body of Christ;" in other words it continues the incarnational ministry begun in the person of Jesus Christ.

2. *The church gathers and scatters.* As a gathered community, the church comes together for worship, education, stewardship, and pastoral care. It then scatters into the world involving itself in evangelism and Zion-building.

3. *Goals and objectives.* As an expression of God's call to be his people in the world, the Saints Church has established six objectives dealing with the theological task, worth of persons, a world church, corporate life, evangelistic life, and Zion.

4. *Restoration.* The church is continually in the process

of restoration, a God-initiated force which acts as a corrective to the continuous tendency toward apostasy.

5. *The call to unity.* The church maintains a unity of purpose in the context of a diversity of individual and group expression.

6. *A covenant people.* Being a member of the church implies life in a state of covenant between the individual and God.

Important Concepts

1. The church does not exist to further its own ends, maintain its own structures, or cater to the desires of its people. Rather it exists to serve God's purposes.

2. Being faithful to God's call requires that the church *constantly* be evaluating its program to ensure that it is not falling away from its purpose.

3. The Saints Church has a unique calling and unique resources. Yet it is also part of the community of Christian churches all of which are trying to be the contemporary expression of Christ in today's world.

4. The church must maintain an appropriate balance between its gathering and scattering endeavors. Over-emphasis or neglect of one or the other will seriously reduce the effectiveness of the church.

5. A clear sense of direction (purpose) as well as well-defined goals and objectives are vital ingredients in the life of the church.

6. Unity in the church means that all individuals work toward a common goal. This can occur even though all persons do not think or act alike.

7. A sense of commitment to covenant provides the basis for a strong fellowship of believers.

Questions for Response

1. How would *you* define the church?

2. What do you think is the most important calling or purpose the church has?

3. Name some specific ways that the church can be the "body of Christ" in your community today.

4. What are some of the consequences that might befall the church that overemphasizes or neglects either the gathering or scattering element?

5. Which of the six objectives on page 98 would you most like to see accomplished? Why? What can you do to contribute? Be specific.

____

____

____

6. What are some tangible evidences of apostasy within the church? Of restoration?

____

____

____

Activities and Research

1. Suggest that each member answer questions 1 and 2 above, individually. Then ask persons to share their responses and allow time for discussion.

2. Invite two persons or teams to debate the issue: The church is the Christian Church *vs.* the church is the Saints Church. The end result here should not be to determine a winning position but rather to bring out the issues and to come to the realization that overemphasis on either extreme is unhealthy.

3. Look over the four gathering functions and two scattering functions found on pages 96 and 97. Using the *Congregational Leaders Handbook* as a reference ask six individuals to each prepare a definition and several good

examples of one function. What can be done to improve the life of the church in each function?

4. Ask a group member to locate a copy of the article "Church Objectives Reviewed and Restated" on pages 3, 4, 5, 55, and 56 of the April 1973 *Saints Herald.* Provide time for this person to facilitate a discussion of World Church goals and objectives. What goals and objectives are there for the region, stake, district, branch, or congregation that you attend? How do they relate to the six objectives in the book?

5. Ask each group member to think of several ways in which they act or believe differently than other members of the group, congregation, or community. Discuss what effects these differences have on group unity. Even though different in some respects, in what things is there unity among the group members?

6. What common project could the group plan and carry out which would be expressive of each individual's commitment to being a covenant people?

Conclusion

Being a member of the church presents all kinds of challenges and opportunities. The key to an effective church is maintaining a sense of togetherness guided by the Holy Spirit. Each person plays a unique role in the community with the opportunity to develop and use talents for the work of God. Being a member of the church is a privilege and carries responsibility to care for one's neighbors.

CHAPTER 10

ALL ARE CALLED

Introduction

The responsibility to which the church is called is a task in which *all* persons are called to participate. Individuals have their unique gifts, talents, and interests. Together they can accomplish much in the name of their Lord. This chapter talks about the common calling of each member and the specific responsibilities of some.

Chapter Overview

The following are the main points covered in this chapter:

1. *The calling of every member.* The basic calling of each member is to assist in the God-given task to be the body of Christ. Each individual also has unique responsibility and the church needs the contribution of each one.

2. *Called to particular responsibilities.* Just as each person has a calling, some have certain functions to fulfill.

3. *The concept and offices of priesthood.* The term priesthood is used to refer to ordination to ministerial responsibilities. Persons are ordained to offices within the Aaronic and Melchisedec priesthoods.

4. *The sacraments of the church.* The Saints Church celebrates the following sacraments: baptism, confirmation, blessing of children, the Lord's Supper, marriage,

administration to the sick, ordination, and patriarchal blessings.

Important Concepts

1. *All* persons have a calling and responsibility within the church to serve others.

2. All responsibilities are of equal importance in the church.

3. The call to priesthood is a call to service in the name of God.

4. The concept of priesthood permits a sharing of responsibilities among a large number of people.

5. Sacraments are symbolic acts of covenant between God and his human creation.

Questions for Response

1. What is your unique calling in the church? Specifically, what contributions can you make to fulfill your calling?

____

____

____

2. What characteristics come to mind when you think of the term "minister"? What are some advantages and disadvantages of the Saints Church system of shared ministerial responsibility?

____

____

3. What are some of the responsibilities that an *un*ordained person can fulfill in the Saints Church?

____

____

____

4. Which of the sacraments of the church have the most significance for you? Why?

____

____

____

Activities and Research

1. Ask someone to read I Corinthians 12 aloud to the group. What does this scripture have to say about unity, diversity, and the calling of every member? Allow time for individuals to express what they think their calling is.

2. Invite participants to discuss the role of education in equipping church members to respond to their calling. Some persons may wish to share how certain educational experiences have benefited them.

3. Using *The Priesthood Manual* and Section 17 of the Doctrine and Covenants ask group members to research the "job descriptions" of the priesthood offices. Each person can take a separate office. Schedule time for the receiving of reports and discussion if interest requires.

4. Your group may be interested in obtaining more information on several or all of the sacraments of the

church. Using *The Priesthood Manual* invite members to gather the information and make reports allowing time for discussion if needed.

5. Women find opportunities for service within the church outside the confines of priesthood responsibilities. What are some ways that women can more meaningfully participate in the life of your congregation? See *Resources for Women's Ministries* for some ideas. What about the contribution of youth?

6. The calling of each person is not only expressed individually. It can also be expressed in group activity. Plan and carry out a group project that will give each member of your group the opportunity to participate meaningfully.

Conclusion

Meaningful participation in the life of the church enhances the worth of the individual. Each person is called and offered the opportunity to respond. In the words of the scripture, "All are called according to the gifts of God unto them" (Doctrine and Covenants 119:8b). The unique contribution of each person in response to God's call makes the body of Christ an effective instrument of salvation in the world.

CHAPTER 11

CHURCH ORGANIZATION

Introduction

To be effective as the body of Christ, the church needs to organize itself and develop certain structures to facilitate its task. The structures of the Saints Church are based on the principle of common consent which provides opportunity for the membership to elect leaders and make policy decisions according to their understanding of what is best for the church.

Chapter Overview

The following are the main points covered in this chapter:

1. *Church administration*. The church is presided over by the First Presidency which supervises six major areas of church affairs: field administration, financial services, administrative services, program services, program planning, and patriarchal ministry.

2. *Legislative functions*. The members participate in decision-making through the legislative process. At the highest level is the World Conference. Legislative sessions are also held at the lower jurisdictional levels.

3. *Judicial process*. Occasionally it becomes necessary to initiate action against individuals in church courts when flagrant violation of church law is apparent. This ministry is always redemptive in intent.

Important Concepts

1. Church government is by the principle of common consent with each member having opportunity to participate in decision-making.

2. Administrative officers are elected or sustained by the people. They hold positions of responsibility designed to serve the needs of the people and to offer guidance in the fulfilling of the church's God-given task.

3. The principle of decentralization makes it possible for decisions to be made close to the point of implementation.

4. Administrative, legislative, and judicial powers are designed to maintain a balance and avoid possible abuses in power.

5. All structures are designed to fulfill important tasks and must remain open to modification where necessary if the church is to adequately respond to its calling.

Questions for Response

1. What concepts or principles of church organization do you see as being most important to the life of the church? Why?

____

____

____

2. How would you characterize the distribution of church membership as seen on the maps and chart on pages 119-121 and 123. To what extent is it rural? Urban? International?

____

____

3. Give examples of the kinds of decisions you think it would be appropriate for (a) congregations and branches, (b) districts, stakes, and regions, (c) national jurisdictions, and (d) the World Church to make that would be consistent with the principle of decentralization.

---

4. What is the objective of judicial process in the church? What might be, in your opinion, sufficient grounds for (a) silencing a minister, (b) excommunicating a member, and (c) expelling a member?

---

5. What are some ways that you could most effectively prepare yourself to participate responsibly in the legislative process of the church?

Activities and Research

1. Using the *Congregational Leaders Handbook* and *Handbook of Church Organization and Administrative Policies and Procedures*, gather more information on the six major areas of the church supervised by the First Presidency. Ask group members to bring reports and facilitate discussion of these areas.

2. Invite your local pastor, presiding elder, district or stake president to tell your group about the organization of the jurisdiction(s) in which you have membership. Have the structures changed during the last five, ten, or twenty years? What changes might be made to make your local church operate more efficiently?

3. Carefully examine the description of the headquarters structure and operations of the First Presidency's staff on pages 115-127. Gather more data as in Activity One if necessary. How can your local church make better use of the services provided by these offices? What services are available from your district, stake, region, or national mission offices?

4. Obtain a recent copy of *Rules and Resolutions* containing all the World Conference resolutions in effect. How would you characterize the church over the last five or ten years based on the issues to which recent resolutions are addressed? One person may research each biennial Conference's resolutions and also include documents from the Doctrine and Covenants for the appropriate years.

Conclusion

Effective church organization is important to the growth and success of the church as it tries to be obedient to God's call. It is the means by which groups of persons organize themselves to accomplish the task. In the Saints Church the members govern the church by common consent, making decisions that they believe will most effectively enable them to do what God requires of them. They elect persons to act on their behalf to give leadership in this important task.

CHAPTER 12

HOW THE CHURCH LIVES

Introduction

Each organization, churches included, has a style of life which identifies it. Certain characteristics are evident when a person joins the fellowship of the Saints Church. These are not so much explainable in terms of purpose, calling, or even organizational structure. Rather they are a matter of behavior. This chapter discusses how the church lives.

Chapter Overview

The following are the main points covered in this chapter:

1. *The church gathered.*
   a. Worship. In the United States and Canada the Saints traditionally meet for worship on Sunday mornings and in many places on Sunday and Wednesday evenings.
   b. Education. In most local churches, the Saints conduct church schools on Sunday mornings.
   c. Pastoral care. More than a specific program, pastoral care is a style of life in the Saints Church.
   d. Stewardship. Individual, family, and corporate church stewardship principles recognize God as creator and persons as responsible for each other's welfare.

2. *The church scattered.*

a. Evangelism. Within the church there are both formal and informal opportunities for evangelistic witness to persons in the communities where the church is located.

b. Zion-building. The Saints care for the communities where they live. They desire to make the structures of society contribute to an environment of wholeness and well-being for all.

Important Concepts

1. The particular activities and life-styles of the many congregations of the Saints Church, although different, have a similarity which is expressed in most of the congregations within the United States and Canada.

2. Worship and education, although carried on in many individual and group settings, are the primary organized activities of the Saints Church.

3. Stewardship and pastoral care are functions which pervade the life of the church and are no less important because they are, for the most part, less formally structured.

4. The gathered life of the church is fruitless unless it gives rise to ministries of outreach.

5. Evangelism is witnessing in word and deed to the lordship of Jesus Christ.

6. Zion-building is the transformation of the societies of the world into the kingdom of God.

Questions for Response

1. What is your experience in public worship in the Saints Church or other churches? Of what value is it *to you?* How

might the worship life of the church be improved?

2. What is your experience in education in the Saints Church or other churches? Of what value is it *to you?* How might the educational life of the church be improved?

3. Give some examples of how you (individually or corporately) care for other people in your church or community. How have others cared for you?

4. Why is stewardship important to the church? How can you be a more responsible steward?

5. List some ways that individuals and groups can witness of Jesus Christ to others.

____

____

____

6. List some ways that individuals and groups can make their community structures more sensitive to the needs of the citizens.

____

____

____

Activities and Research

1. Attend a worship service of the Saints Church as a group. Afterwards discuss what went on at the service. What criteria of evaluation did you use? How might the service be improved if it were to be repeated?

2. Evaluate the formal educational program of your congregation. Are objectives stated or implied? Are they being accomplished? Does your group find the objectives and procedures appropriate and effective?

3. Ask members of the group to try to recall their reactions the first time they went into a congregation of the Saints Church. Persons who can't recall may think of someone else's first reaction that they have heard. Allow time for sharing and discussion of these first reactions.

4. Ask members of the class to read philosophical statements of the six congregational life functions. Sources are *Called and Sent* and *Congregational Leaders Handbook*. Are these statements consistent with the experiences of the persons who have done the reading and the other members of the group? How can what actually goes on be improved?

5. Ask persons who joined the Saints Church as adults or who were not "born and raised in the church" to recall what features of the church were most responsible for their joining. All members may wish to try to determine what about the Saints Church would attract them today if they were not already members. Perhaps group members know persons who have recently joined the church and could relate their feelings.

Conclusion

Membership in the Saints Church is important to those who are members. It is important to different individuals for varying reasons. The life of the church offers a sense of identity, solidarity, and hope to persons who are joined together in a common cause.

CHAPTER 13

WHERE IS THE WORLD GOING?

Introduction

We all think about the future to some degree. This is true both in the realm of planning for what we might do or what might happen to us and in terms of our general outlook toward the future. The Saints Church supports the Christian affirmation that there is *hope* in the future. This hope is based on God's victory over evil in the person of the resurrected Christ.

Chapter Overview

The following are the main points covered in this chapter:

1. *How do we feel about the future?* The future can be viewed basically in one of two ways. It can be seen as corrupt and without possibility of improvement or it can be seen as having hope and potential for becoming better.

2. *What does the gospel say about the future?* God assures us that the future is in his hands and that it is moving toward the realization of his kingdom prophesied by Jesus Christ.

3. *How can we live in hope?* By placing our faith in God we can live in confidence that in spite of adverse circumstances God is the victor.

Important Concepts

1. Reflection on the future is part of the experience of each one of us. This concern, however, needs to be placed in the perspective of living each moment fully in the present.

2. How we *feel* about the future cannot determine it or change it. This is possible only by active participation in the present.

3. We all experience adverse circumstances in our lives. These should be seen, however, against the backdrop of God's supreme victory over evil which gives us the strength to live through adversity.

4. God's coming kingdom is not a wished-for ideal. It is the certainty toward which history is unalterably moving.

5. God's world is a unified whole that cannot be legitimately divided into sacred and secular spheres.

6. Faith regarding the future is not so much knowing the unknown as it is believing in God and that he can be trusted.

Questions for Response

1. What specific decisions have you made today or this week which have implications for the future? Which have short-term implications? Which long-term?

---

2. What is your overall view of the future at this time? Why do you hold this view? Are you satisfied with your present view? Why or why not?

3. What does the Christian gospel say to your view of the future? Do you *really believe* that God is forever victorious and that his kingdom will be a reality?

4. Give examples of the tendency to separate "secular" and "sacred" elements of life. How can you avoid this tendency?

5. What are the limitations and problems in developing concepts about the future that are too specific?

Activities and Research

1. Bring copies of recent newspapers to class and ask group members to find evidences of how people today view the future. What major themes emerge? How are they similar to the views held by group members?

2. Ask one person to read paragraph eleven "the kingdom of God" on pages 162-171 of *Exploring the Faith.* This person can make a report and facilitate a discussion on the subject.

3. Use a Bible concordance and ask group members to look up the many references to the kingdom of God found in the four gospels. What appears to be Jesus' view of the future?

4. As a group develop specific plans for ways that you can act today to bring about a better future for yourselves, your families, your congregations, and your communities.

Conclusion

We must choose how we view the future. We can affirm with hope that the future is in God's hands and that we will do all we can to assist in the accomplishment of his purposes. Or we can throw up our hands in despair. Christ calls us to participate with him in the coming kingdom. Such participation can give meaning to our lives and enrich all of our relationships.

CHAPTER 14

EVANGELISM

Introduction

Evangelism is witnessing to the reality of Jesus Christ and that through him God acts to save each individual and the world. Evangelism is the natural expression of people who have been grasped by the love of God. It is the sharing of the gospel with persons with whom we come in contact.

Chapter Overview

The following are the main points covered in this chapter:

1. *Witnessing of Jesus Christ.* It is to the reality of Jesus Christ that we witness. He represents God's initiative in our lives.

2. *The evangelistic life.* Evangelism is a style of life. We become evangelistic by thrusting ourselves into the midst of life, where people are.

3. *Newness of life.* God offers us new life in Christ. Two understandings that guide the life of the disciple are that the love of God is the center of life and that the worth of persons through God's grace becomes the focus of all relationships.

Important Concepts

1. Sharing the gospel with others is a *natural* outgrowth of the corporate life of the Saints.

2. The essence of evangelistic witness is that God has acted in our lives. This is the good news, i.e. the gospel.

3. Individuals or the church cannot experience salvation in isolation from the rest of the world.

4. Evangelism is as much a style of *life* as it is what we *tell* other people.

5. The two basic understandings on which the evangelistic message is founded is the existence of a loving God and the worth of every person.

Questions for Response

1. The gospel is "good news." Have you perceived this good news in your life? If so, explain how and when.

____

____

____

2. What is your "testimony of Jesus Christ"? What testimonies of other persons can you remember?

____

____

____

3. Why is it so important to be disciples "in association with other disciples"? Why can't we do it on our own?

4. What hints about being effective evangelists can we get from the life of Jesus?

5. Give some examples of how you can act as "leaven" in your neighborhood or community.

6. Look at the two primary understandings and eight basic affirmations on pages 155 and 156. Which of these do you feel are particularly important? Why?

Activities and Research

1. Invite as many persons in the group as wish to share brief testimonies of the reality of Christ in their lives. Then allow time for observations regarding the testimonies. Be

careful not to permit criticism or judgment of the validity of each other's testimonies.

2. As a group plan and implement a short-range evangelism program which can be carried out by the group during the study of the book. Make sure that the program goes beyond words to a strong base of *action*. After it is completed, spend a short time in evaluation.

3. Evaluate the life-style of your congregation, giving attention to the extent to which it is evangelistic. How can your congregation become more evangelistic? What can members of your group do about it?

4. Base a group discussion on the two concepts: God's love as the center of life and the worth of all persons as the focus of all relationships. It could be said that there are two principles of the gospel. How can these two concepts become the base of evangelism in the church?

5. Have each member of the group choose a different one of the basic affirmations on pages 155 and 156. Schedule time for persons to report how they see their affirmations being expressed in the evangelistic life of the church.

6. See *Evangelism: The Spirit of Community* (Herald House, 1974) for additional activity suggestions on the subject of evangelism.

Conclusion

A church which does not share the basis of its life with others will surely die. All members of the church have both the responsibility and the opportunity to share in the evangelistic expression of the church. It is the natural response to the love of God in our lives. Evangelism is the witness to others of Jesus Christ who is the center and foundation of our faith.

CHAPTER 15

ZION

Introduction

The Saints have always emphasized the importance of the kingdom of God. This has been expressed particularly in the concept of *Zion* as God's kingdom on earth. Zion represents an opportunity for persons to give tangible expression to their ideals and to structure their communities in ways consistent with what they understand to be God's will.

Chapter Overview

The following are the main points covered in this chapter:

1. *Zion as place.* The Saints believe that Zion-building can and should occur in all areas of the world. Independence, Missouri, U.S.A., is nevertheless looked at as the Center Place.

2. *Zion as a condition.* Zionic living reflects the love of God among people with utmost regard for the worth of each individual.

3. *Zion as a process.* Zion is an endeavor that is continuous. It is never complete at any point in time.

Important Concepts

1. Although Independence, Missouri, has an important and unique role as the Center Place, Zionic endeavors are giving meaning to the lives of people in many places throughout the world.

2. Zion as an earthly expression of God's kingdom is directly related to the everyday structures of our societies which it seeks to transform.

3. The principle of mutual love and concern for each other is the foundational condition that identifies Zionic living.

4. Each culture and subculture has its unique and important contribution to make to the establishment of Zion.

5. Zion is always in the process of becoming. To the extent that Zionic conditions prevail now, Zion is already here. Yet it is not fully here; its fuller expression is still to be seen.

6. Zion-building is a *corporate* endeavor. All persons can share and their assistance is needed.

Questions for Response

1. Why do you suppose the Saints have stressed the idea of God's kingdom as being "in this world"? Is this view important to you? Why or why not?

____

____

____

2. What is the potential for your community to become part of the kingdom of God? What can you do to bring this about?

____

____

____

____

3. What would appear to you to be the unique functions of a "center place" of Zionic development?

____

____

____

____

4. To what extent do Zionic *conditions* exist in the communities where you have lived? How can you personally improve these conditions?

____

____

____

____

5. What characteristics of a Zionic condition are important to you? Are there some that are not listed on pages 161-163?

____

____

____

____

6. What kinds of individual and group actions do you think would contribute most to the process of Zion-building (a) in your community, (b) in your country, (c) world wide?

____

____

____

____

Activities and Research

1. Ask group members to read selections from the book of articles on Zion titled *Readings on Concepts of Zion* (Herald House, 1973). Allow time for reporting and discussion.

2. Participants could research the references to the term Zion in the Three Standard Books. Particular things to look for could be (a) the Old Testament meaning of Zion and (b) the changing image of Zion in the Latter Day Saint tradition (see Doctrine and Covenants).

3. Another research project could involve one or more group members in locating examples of specific Zionic endeavors of the Saints Church. The early volumes of Church History describe gathering experiences at Kirtland, Independence, and Nauvoo, for example.

4. Arrange for a three-sided debate as follows: One person or a team could support the position that Zion is a *place*. A second person or team could take the position that Zion is a *condition* and the third that Zion is a *process*. The result will, hopefully, be a greater appreciation for all three aspects of the Zionic endeavor.

5. Plan and conduct a modest group project aimed at building Zion in your community. After the project is completed spend some time in evaluation.

6. Brainstorm a list of ways that your congregation or community group could Zionize your community. Make plans for how some of these can be implemented or at least given further consideration.

Conclusion

Zion is the direction in which God is leading the world. He invites all persons to enlist in his work. By perceiving where God is at work in our communities and becoming involved with him, we can speed the process of Zion-building and therefore enrich the lives of persons around us.

CHAPTER 16

STEWARDSHIP

Introduction

The concept of stewardship is based on a belief in God as creator of the universe and all that is in it. As human beings we are stewards over those things which are at our disposal. Our responsibility is to use what we have, not just for our own benefit but also for the benefit of others.

Chapter Overview

1. *Who are stewards?* All persons are stewards whether they acknowledge it or not. This also applies to groups of people.

2. *Over what are we stewards?* We are stewards over all of our resources. In addition to life itself, we exercise stewardship responsibility over material possessions, skills, health, time, the gospel, and other things.

3. *What is responsible stewardship?* In responsible stewardship we recognize our dependence on God and that all that we have is *not* the result of our own efforts. In so doing we consider the needs of others as well as our own needs.

4. *Our corporate stewardship.* Families, church congregations, and other groups also have stewardship responsibilities.

Important Concepts

1. God is creator and provider of all.

2. All people are stewards.

3. We are expected to exercise responsible stewardship over all that we have.

4. Responsible stewardship requires that we provide not only for our own needs but also for other persons who have needs.

5. It is important that persons develop an "increase" in their financial, time, skill, and other resources in order to provide for their own security and for other persons.

6. The church as a corporate body is just as responsible and accountable for the use of its resources as are individuals and families.

Questions for Response

1. Enumerate the basic categories of resources that you have. Over which ones has your stewardship been less than adequate in your opinion? What can you do about it?

____

____

____

2. Why is it difficult sometimes to acknowledge that God is creator and giver of all? Give some specific examples of times when you have encountered this difficulty.

____

____

3. Examine the concepts of inheritance, increase, surplus, and storehouse on pages 170-171. Why is each important?

4. What is your first reaction to the financial law described on pages 171 and 172? Could you comply with this law? What sacrifices would you have to make? What would be the benefits?

5. What are some specific ways in which you can use your time and skills more responsibly?

6. How can you better contribute to the corporate endeavor of the local congregation?

7. In what ways can your local congregation or other community group be more responsible in the use of its resources?

Activities and Research

1. Ask one person to read paragraph ten, pages 152-161, titled "Stewardship" in *Exploring the Faith* (Herald House, 1970). This person can present a report and facilitate a discussion of stewardship.

2. Look at paragraph ten on page 212 of the book. Analyze this paragraph and suggest that the group rewrite it in its own words.

3. Ask members of the group to think of one special resource that they feel a special sense of stewardship over. Ask individuals to share with the group how they see their resource being used responsibly. This could be done in the spirit of offering in a worship setting.

4. Suggest that the group think of ways that your local congregation can be more responsible in the use of its resources. This will probably imply setting of goals, determining strategy, evaluation, etc. For materials on this subject see the bibliography on pages 216-219 of the book.

5. How might a storehouse be established by your congregation? What would be principles for its operation? If it seems feasible make plans to implement this important concept.

6. See *Stewardship: The Response of My People* (Herald

House, 1976) for additional activity suggestions on the subject of stewardship.

Conclusion

"Stewardship is the response of my people to the ministry of my Son and is required alike of all those who seek to build the kingdom" (Doctrine and Covenants 147:5a). This statement clearly describes the nature of stewardship as our response to God's free gift of his Son. It also indicates that all persons should accept responsibility if they are to be Christ's disciples. Using what we have responsibly can add meaning to our lives and enrich the lives of others.

CHAPTER 17

WHAT IT MEANS TO BE A MEMBER

Introduction

Membership in the Saints Church is meaningful for each person who holds it. The significance of membership is not easily communicated to those who are not members. Nevertheless this chapter attempts to summarize the significance of the church with the hope that persons unfamiliar with it may gain some insights into why members find it meaningful.

Chapter Overview

1. *The significance of history.* History is the filter through which the past is seen. From the past we can learn important lessons for living in the present.

2. *The significance of belief.* Beliefs help define the nature of a community of people. On the other hand, belief is an individual matter.

3. *The significance of organization.* Structures, offices, procedures, and other organizational elements of the church are important. However, they must be flexible and adaptable to the demands of changing times.

4. *The significance of practice.* How people behave individually and corporately reveals a lot about them. The life-style of the Saints Church is characterized by diversity within a basic unity of purpose.

Important Concepts

1. History represents human *interpretations* of past events. It is impossible to accurately recover the past.

2. A basic familiarity with the past equips persons and groups for sound decision making in the present.

3. The Saints have always affected and been affected by their cultural surroundings.

4. Belief is an intensely personal matter but common beliefs lend identity to groups.

5. The Saints have always avoided solidifying their beliefs into creeds. However, statements of belief are used to summarize beliefs common to the membership of the church.

6. "Form follows function" is a sound organizational principle which ensures adaptability to changing needs.

7. The Saints have a style of life which unifies them in their common calling while each individual has unique interests and contributions.

Questions for Response

1. Write a brief statement to indicate what membership in the Saints Church (or other organization) means to you.

____

____

____

2. Look back over your own personal, family, or community history and identify what meaning it has for you.

3. What are your religious beliefs? Why does it matter what you believe?

4. Give some examples of how church organization needs to be flexible and sometimes needs to be changed.

5. What are the essential ingredients of unity in the Saints Church?

Activities and Research

1. Ask a group member to summarize the content of Chapter One of the book. What do members think are the most significant aspects (not necessarily single events) of the history of the Saints Church?

2. As a group, analyze the statement of belief on pages 210-215 of the book. Which paragraphs, sentences, or concepts do group members think are most significant to the church today?

3. Ask one participant to review the content of Chapter Eleven in the book. What do persons think are the most significant parts of church organization? Where does the church need to be more flexible in its organization? Why?

4. Ask each class member to share a brief testimony of an experience of visiting a congregation away from home. What similarities were experienced? What differences?

5. Discuss the question of tolerance. What differences among members is your group, congregation, or the church as a whole willing to tolerate? What differences are *not* tolerated? Why?

Conclusion

Membership in the Saints Church may be significant to various members of the church for different reasons. The important thing is a belief in and dedication to what the church is attempting to accomplish. God wants us to be responsive to his call. The Saints are a group of people who find meaning in this response.

CHAPTER 18

PERSONAL IDENTITY

Introduction

The gospel of Jesus Christ gives each person identity as a new being. In Christ our brokenness is made whole and our empty lives find meaning. In the midst of our struggle with the questions of who we are and what our roles in society are we are strengthened by the assurance that we are children of God and loved by him unconditionally.

Chapter Overview

1. *A belief one stands by.* An important part of our identity is our belief in God.

2. *Certain definite ways of responding to life.* The mark of Christians is that they respond to life's situations in the light of the gospel.

3. *Of loving other people.* By knowing, accepting, and loving ourselves we are empowered to love others.

4. *Of serving God.* By serving our fellow beings we are at the same time serving God.

5. *One's witness to truth in one's life.* Our lives witness to what we have come to perceive as truth.

6. *Devotion.* Honest reflection in meditation and prayer is an integral part of the life of the disciple.

Important Concepts

1. God's unconditional love invites our response.

2. Encounter with the gospel (i.e. Jesus Christ) changes our lives.

3. God grants each person a new identity and lives are infused with meaning.

4. The gospel helps persons become aware of who they are.

5. Belief is grounded in God and not in finite things.

6. The gospel conditions our responses to people and to situations. Fear and arrogance are replaced by confidence and humility.

7. The Christian lives always in love.

8. Service to God and service to others are inseparable.

9. Prayer and meditation are important to honest self-assessment.

Questions for Response

1. Why is it so difficult for us to believe that God loves all persons regardless of their "misdeeds and misplaced ideals"?

---

2. What might be tangible evidences of a person being made new through encounter with Christ?

---

3. What are your marks of identity (a) as a person, (b) as a Christian? To what extent do you think these marks are observed by other people?

4. In a sentence, state what belief you "stand by."

5. How do you tend to respond when you are (a) irritated, (b) inconvenienced, (c) exposed to something new?

6. Do you always express love toward (a) family and friends, (b) acquaintances, (c) strangers? If not, why not?

7. Specifically, how can you get to know yourself better through a more meaningful devotional life?

____

____

____

Activities and Research

1. Ask group members to spend five minutes individually trying to determine their most obvious marks of identification (behavioral rather than physical). Then divide the group into pairs and ask persons to try to determine their neighbor's most obvious marks of identification. Allow time for persons to share their observations in pairs. How similar was each person's own determinations to the determination of his or her partner?

2. Using a Bible concordance, research New Testament references to newness of life (including "new man," "new being," etc.). Pool your findings and determine how your lives individually and collectively can be made new by Christ.

3. Ask six group members to carefully choose and study one of the six subsections of this chapter as identified in the chapter overview. Then allow these persons to make a brief presentation followed by group discussion.

4. Give group members opportunity to bear their testimonies of the power of Christ in their lives or make a statement of intent with regard to becoming more closely identified with Christ through active discipleship.

Conclusion

The gospel of Jesus Christ gives meaning and purpose to life. The disciple bears the marks of identity of a Christian. The truly converted follower is one who is changed and who has experienced newness of life. The invitation and opportunity for response is offered by God to *all* persons.

CHAPTER 19

ETHICS: DECISIONS, DECISIONS, DECISIONS

Introduction

Each person is faced with making decisions. There are several different approaches to decision-making. For the Christian, "right" is influenced by belief in God and the exemplary life-style of Jesus Christ. The gospel does not eliminate the need to make decisions, nor does it make decision-making easier. It does however, give us a context for making decisions.

Chapter Overview

1. *Rules.* This is the approach that suggests that right and wrong can be determined by consulting certain agreed-upon rules or laws.

2. *Good sense.* This approach suggests that the best foundation for wise decision-making is the use of good sense and rational thinking.

3. *Relationships.* This approach sees persons as more important than rules and examines each situation separately.

4. *Which approach?* Each of the three approaches mentioned has its advantages but each also has its dangers.

5. *Some general principles.* The Saints Church has emphasized several basic ethical principles which focus on

the worth of persons, obedience to God, and peace and justice in society.

Important Concepts

1. All persons are faced with making decisions and each of us searches for a base to inform our decision-making.

2. For the Christian, the gospel of Jesus Christ is basic to decision-making.

3. All ethical approaches have their advantages and their limitations. No one approach is adequate.

4. Persons have to decide for themselves which approaches will be given greatest emphasis.

5. In ethical decisions it is important to remember that each person has special worth and uniqueness in the sight of God and that persons should not take oppressive action toward anyone.

Questions for Response

1. List the three most significant ethical decisions that you made during the last week. What guiding principles helped you decide the way you did?

____

____

____

2. What is the most important belief or reality on which you base your decisions?

____

____

3. What do you see as the major advantages and disadvantages of RULES ethics?

4. What do you see as the major advantages and disadvantages of GOOD SENSE ethics?

5. What do you see as the major advantages and disadvantages of RELATIONSHIPS ethics?

6. Which of the three ethical positions described do you tend to emphasize most? Why?

7. What can make you more responsible in your decision-making?

____

____

____

Activities and Research

1. Assign persons or teams to each of the three approaches to ethics described in the book and conduct a three-way debate. The outcome should be a greater appreciation of the need for all three approaches rather than the declaration of a winner.

2. Examine the paragraphs of World Conference Resolution 1085 on page 199. Ask one or two persons to concentrate on each of the four paragraphs. Allow time for these persons to talk about how helpful the guidance is and to involve the whole group in a discussion of the implications.

3. Invite group members to tell of particularly difficult decisions they had to make. What might have been the consequences of deciding differently than they did?

4. As a group work on defining some procedures that would enable persons to be more sensitive to the three general principles found on pages 198-200.

Conclusion

Ethics is primarily a matter of free and grateful response to God for his gift to us in Jesus Christ. The heart of ethics is in the gospel. On one hand we are obligated to God for all that he has given us. On the other hand, we have been set free by the salvation we have been given in Jesus Christ. The goal of ethics is to make decisions which are both responsible and free. This is possible only by the grace of God. The essence of ethics is love. God is love. He is creating us now in his likeness and wants us to learn how to become loving creatures.

CHAPTER 20

THE SAINTS CHURCH, THE RELIGIOUS COMMUNITY, AND THE WORLD

Introduction

The Saints Church does not exist in isolation. It functions alongside other denominations in the Christian community and alongside other institutions in the broader religious community. The church also exists in the world. This chapter explores these relationships.

Chapter Overview

1. *The church and the religious community.* The Saints affirm the uniqueness of their calling but also acknowledge that they share the responsibility for God's work with others.

2. *The church and Mormonism.* Although they both emerged from a common beginning, the Saints Church and Mormon church differ widely in belief, organization, and practice.

3. *The church and the world.* The Saints acknowledge an interest in and responsibility for the world which is the arena of God's action.

Important Concepts

1. The Saints Church does not live in isolation from other religious and social institutions.

2. The Saints Church is different from all other religious bodies. However, it shares with them the common task of being God's presence in the world.

3. The Saints seek to cooperate with other institutions which are seeking a better world.

4. The differences between the Mormon and Saints churches need not be a source of antagonism but rather a reflection of religious diversity.

5. The church is called to be "in the world but not of it," bringing God's redeeming presence to those whom he seeks to save.

Questions for Response

1. Why is it important for Saints to recognize both their differences and their similarities with respect to other Christians?

___

___

___

2. What are the advantages and disadvantages of cooperating with other churches in doing God's work?

___

___

___

3. What do you know about the Mormon church? How

might both the Mormon church and Saints Church benefit from a closer relationship?

4. What are some of the advantages and disadvantages of the church being apart from the world most of the time?

5. What are some of the advantages and disadvantages of the church identifying closely with the world most of the time?

Activities and Research

1. Ask each member of the group to do a little research into the belief and practices of another Christian or non-Christian denomination in your community. Allow time for reports on things that the Saints Church can learn from these other churches.

2. As a group, plan one or more ways in which your local congregation can cooperate with other churches in the community in doing God's work.

3. As a group, investigate organizations in your community that may have resources to offer the church. Examples might be schools, libraries, Chamber of Commerce, civic groups.

4. Invite a member of the Mormon church to come to the group and share a little about Mormon beliefs. It is important that this be a learning experience and not a time for argumentation.

5. If this is the last meeting of the group, plan a short worship experience that will involve all members of the group in some way.

Conclusion

The Saints stand unified in their witness to God's love in their lives. They are dedicated to the building of God's kingdom on earth. This requires being "in the world but not of the world." The Saints are pleased to be a part of God's work and extend the invitation to all to participate.